D1234217

THE JUDICIAL DECISION

THE
JUDICIAL DECISION

Toward a Theory of Legal Justification

Richard A. Wasserstrom

STANFORD UNIVERSITY PRESS

STANFORD, CALIFORNIA, 1961

LONDON: OXFORD UNIVERSITY PRESS

STANFORD UNIVERSITY PRESS
STANFORD, CALIFORNIA

LONDON: OXFORD UNIVERSITY PRESS

© 1961 by the Board of Trustees of the
Leland Stanford Junior University

Library of Congress Catalog Card Number: 61-6535

Printed in the United States of America

To my wife, Phyllis

Acknowledgments

Earlier versions of this work were read by a number of people, all of whom provided needed and apt suggestions and criticisms. This book is a better book than it would otherwise have been because of the encouragement and aid they so generously furnished. Thus, while taking care to absolve them of any responsibility for the defects that remain, I gratefully acknowledge a substantial debt to the following persons:

Professors William K. Frankena, Paul Henle, and Carl Cohen of the Philosophy Department of the University of Michigan; and Professor Spencer L. Kimball of the University of Michigan Law School

My father, Alfred H. Wasserstrom

Professor Ernest Nagel of the Philosophy Department of Columbia University

Professor Herbert Morris of the Philosophy Department and School of Law of the University of California at Los Angeles

Professor Leo Levin of the University of Pennsylvania Law School.

R.A.W.

Palo Alto
February 7, 1961

Contents

Contents

1

Introduction

To observe that any complex society requires a successfully functioning legal system is surely to take notice of a commonplace. And to report that one of the essential functions of any legal system is to decide cases is even more certainly to state a tautology. But it is one thing to recognize that a society must have a legal system and that the legal system must inevitably decide cases; it is something else again to analyze the procedures that might be used in the process of adjudication. The latter undertaking raises, in one form or another, almost all of the more perplexing problems of legal philosophy. For inextricably related to any of the substantial questions with which legal philosophers have been concerned is the question of how the controversies presented to the legal system for adjudication ought to be resolved.

It is more than a little surprising, therefore, to discover that the task of examining the possible procedures by which a legal system either should or could decide cases has on the whole been neglected by legal philosophers. To the extent to which the nature of the judicial process has been subjected to explicit and thorough analysis, the context of the inquiry has usually been empirical rather than normative. Studies have been made of the kinds of criteria to which courts have in fact appealed, of the weight which respective courts accord to differing "sources of law," and of the diverse factors which influence the course of judicial decisions, often without the judge's awareness. But when raised at all, the question of what would constitute a desirable decision procedure has been answered only indirectly. Legal philosophers have stated, often imprecisely, the reasons why they regard certain kinds of procedures as undesirable. They have been more reticent and even less exact when the subsequent specification of their own affirmative proposals has then become relevant.

The failure to speak directly to the issue of what would constitute an optimum procedure of adjudication has given rise to several seriously ambiguous theses of contemporary legal philosophies. Because the fundamental tenets of these theses have remained unclarified, an explication and evaluation of their relevance to and significance for this question of the nature of a desirable decision procedure is difficult. In large measure, this inquiry is an attempt to sort out the various possible claims of recent legal philosophies and to subject them to critical analysis and evaluation.

Described in extremely general terms, much of the history of legal philosophy during the twentieth century is the story of the rise of what have been regarded as new jurisprudential movements. Dissatisfaction with the "older" approaches of analytic natural law and historical jurisprudence, and in particular with the espousal of a "logical," "conceptual," or "mechanical" procedure of judicial decision making, led legal philosophers and law teachers to demand innovations in legal thought. In Europe, the theory of "free decision" and the school of a "jurisprudence of interests" rose to prominence. In America, the "call" for a realistic, a sociological, or a pragmatic jurisprudence did not fall on deaf ears. But though the call was loud, it was often far from clear.

Indeed, there was and still is a significant ambiguity in the very names of many of these proposed new approaches. The plea is made, for example, for a realistic jurisprudence, a sociological jurisprudence, a jurisprudence of interests, or a pragmatic or experimental jurisprudence. But what does this require? Is this a request for an *analysis of* any given legal system in accordance with the canons of realism, the tools and findings of sociology, or the method of inquiry characteristic of pragmatism? If so, if we may understand these "schools" to be suggesting ways by which to study a legal system, they are surely proposing a legitimate enterprise. But they are not thereby seeking to concern themselves with the question of how any legal system ought to decide cases. On the other hand, the proponents of these several positions can also be understood to be prescribing the *manner in which* some or all of the segments of the legal system ought to reach their decisions. They might be saying, in effect, that a court should be realistic in rendering a verdict, that the content of sociological inquiries and the methodology of the sociologists ought to be utilized by the judiciary and the legislature in the performance of their functions, or that a judge should be pragmatic in his adjudication of the cases that come before him. Despite the obvious divergence between these two possible programs—the one relevant to a study of the law, the other relevant to development within the law—this distinction has far too seldom been made explicit. No doubt proponents have envisioned the implementation of both activities—have believed, for instance, that the legal system should be studied realistically *and* that cases ought to be decided realistically. But the failure to separate the disparate import of these two proposals has only succeeded in obscuring the fact that arguments which support the one may well be inappropriate to the other.

Since this study is concerned with the problem of how courts ought to decide cases, the contributions of the "schools" of legal philosophy alluded to above become relevant only if they are interpreted as suggesting a procedure or set of procedures by which cases ought to be decided. But even when restricted to this more narrow topic, the claims of the adherents to a realistic, a sociological, or an experimental jurisprudence remain imprecise. Almost everyone insists, for example, that a "mechanical" or "logical" judicial decision procedure will not permit the legal system to fulfill its proper function. It is agreed that if the legal system is to perform successfully those tasks which it ought to perform in contemporary society, it cannot and should not attempt to decide cases by the "sterile" application of general legal rules to the facts of particular cases.

It is this belief that a "mechanical" or "logical" decision procedure is undesirable which is ambiguous in its usual form. For example, the disparagement of a reliance upon logic might be construed as a means of pointing out that the canons of logic are essentially concerned with the conditions of formal correctness as opposed to material desirability. The point, that is, might be simply that logic is concerned with the relations between propositions rather than the content of the propositions themselves. Thus the call for something like a realistic jurisprudence might be a request for the recognition of this important fact, and an insistence that the canons of logic be supplemented by a continued revision of the content of legal rules in the light of realistic, sociological, or pragmatic considerations.

The "call" for a new jurisprudence might, however, mean something quite different, and it doubtless has to many of its staunchest adherents. Concomitant with the deprecation of a logical decision procedure has been the insistence that some essentially nonlogical decision procedure should be systematically introduced and employed by the judiciary. Although this proposal is seldom made very clearly, its apparent intent is that cases ought to be decided by the employment of a method which lacks either some or all of those characteristics most often associated with a rational resolution of a problematic situation. Just as the disapproval of a logical decision process might be nothing more than the recognition that an independent set of criteria is needed to evaluate the content and import of legal rules, so too the rejection of "rationalism" or "conceptualism" in the law might be a proposal that cases be decided in a manner markedly different from one that would be termed a reasoned adjudication of pending litigation. Thus there is a serious lack of clarity not only in the basis of the attack upon a logical decision process, but also in the proposal to substitute a realistic or sociological method for deciding cases.

In still a different context, the attack upon a logical decision procedure could quite reasonably be construed as a recognition of the fact that a legal rule cannot be "logically" applied to fact situations that the rule itself does not control. If a "new" or "unprovided" case arises, there is no legal rule which inexorably applies to that case and dictates its solution. But here, too, the denial of a "mechanical" jurisprudence has at times implied something more far-reaching. Not only, it is suggested, is there nothing inexorable about the application of existing rules to novel fact situations, but there is also a sense in which it is meaningless to talk about the applicability of rules of law to any fact situations, be they novel or common.

This study, then, has a twofold purpose: It is an endeavor to delineate more precisely the nature and persuasiveness of the continued attack upon a rationalistic or deductive decision procedure; and it is, further, an attempt to evaluate the alternative programs of judicial decision which have been suggested or evoked by the rejection of a "logical" decision procedure.

Such an undertaking has certain inherent difficulties. For one need not be overly familiar with the intricacies of the law to realize that any legal system is amazingly complex; so complex, in fact, that a serious dilemma is posed for anyone who seeks to discuss it. On the one hand, a feeling for the richness of legal experience can be retained only at the price of a certain vagueness of discourse. On the other hand, the pursuit of clarity leads almost inevitably to the introduction of a simplified and hence artificial context of discussion. I have tried to keep the focus of this analysis somewhere between these two extremes. Certain assumptions about the legal system have been made, and these assumptions serve to distinguish the legal system I discuss from the systems that actually exist. Whenever I have been conscious of them, I have tried to make my assumptions explicit. I have also, however, by using illustrative cases and related materials, sought to talk about a legal system that is similar in important respects to the legal system with which I am most familiar—the Anglo-American legal system.

There are various ways in which one might explore both the particular problem of what is wrong with a rationalistic decision process and the more general problem of what process courts ought to use. I have chosen to develop the inquiry by examining in turn several decision procedures that courts might employ. Throughout most of this study I shall be considering three distinctive "ideal" legal decision procedures, seeking to delineate their most important characteristics and to evaluate the consequences of their employment by a judiciary.

There are at least three senses in which these procedures can be said to be ideal. First, as suggested above, they are ideal in that they are not presented as empirically accurate delineations of

the way in which all courts of any legal system have decided all or
even most cases. But, at the same time, they are ideal in the sense
that they illustrate some of the most essential characteristics of
decision procedures that courts have often employed. And finally,
they are ideal in a third and most significant sense in that they are
offered as embodying those features which, some have argued, a
legal decision procedure ought to possess.

Although each of these three procedures differs from one or
both of the other procedures in several respects, each can be distinguished from all the others by virtue of its employment of what
I shall term a distinctive *rule of decision*. That is to say, apart from
the other elements which it may uniquely possess, each procedure
is distinguished by its use of a special kind of rule—a rule that
specifies what in general is to count as a good reason for deciding
any case in a certain way. The operational differences occasioned
by the unequivocal employment of any one of these rules of
decision serve as the analytic focus for the evaluation of each
procedure.

The first of the three ideal procedures can be called the *procedure of precedent*, because its rule of decision prescribes that
all particular cases are to be decided by an appeal to the relevant,
extant legal rule, i.e., to precedent. Thus in a legal system in
which such a rule of decision is uniquely operative, the necessary
and sufficient conditions for the adjudication of any case would
consist in a finding that the result is dictated by some controlling
precedent.

A judicial decision procedure employing this rule alone has
been rejected by many legal philosophers on the grounds that
it is incompatible with the function or functions that a mature
legal system ought to fulfill. Indeed, this may be the procedure
that legal philosophers have had in mind when they have talked
disparagingly about a "logical" or "mechanical" method of decision. Because legal rules play such an important role in a procedure based on precedent, many philosophers have apparently
also thought that legal rules ought to have no place in the legal
decision process and that, therefore, cases ought to be decided
without reference to them.

Many of the proposals for an alternative to precedent are delineated in the discussion of the second of the two ideal procedures, which I have called the *procedure of equity* because it insists that individual cases be decided by appealing to that which is just or equitable for the particular case. The decision procedures which have been offered as exemplifying an equitable procedure have taken several forms and have, correspondingly, raised various problems. But here too, although differing from one another in important ways, all of the equitable procedures considered are at least alike in their insistence that the necessary and sufficient condition for adjudicating a particular case consists in a finding that the result reached was the most just or equitable vis-à-vis the parties before the court. Thus, rather than deciding cases in accordance with precedent, the equitable decision procedures decide cases by appealing to the merits of the particular controversy before the court at any given time and place.

The third procedure, related to the procedures of both precedent and equity, embodies certain distinctive attributes of each while eliminating some of the more serious deficiencies of both. Speaking oversimply, the rule of decision that distinguishes this procedure resembles the rule of the precedential procedure in that an appeal to a legal rule (or something like a legal rule) is a necessary condition for deciding a case in a certain way. It is unlike the precedential rule of decision in that this appeal is not a sufficient condition for any particular decision. And the rule of decision is like the equitable rule of decision in that considerations of justice are directly relevant to the justification of any decision. But it is unlike the equitable rule in that the justice of a legal rule (or something analogous to a legal rule), rather than the justice of the particular decision, is the sufficient condition for a particular decision. For want of a more appropriate name, this procedure is called a *two-level procedure* of justification.

Having said that the two-level decision procedure succeeds in avoiding the more serious weaknesses of the precedential and equitable procedures, one would like to assert as well that this procedure is free from difficulties of its own. Unfortunately, it is not. For as I shall endeavor to point out in the discussion of this pro-

cedure in Chapter 7, it improves upon the other two procedures
only at the price of becoming imprecise, as a procedure, at certain
crucial points. Thus, it is not literary modesty but rather philosophical uncertainty which leads me to subtitle this study *"Toward
A Theory of Legal Justification."* If the work succeeds at all, it does
so not because it presents any definitive theory of how all cases
ought to be decided, but because it lays bare some of the implications of certain of the more obvious ways in which courts might
go about deciding cases.

Before undertaking an analysis of any of these procedures, it is
desirable to make explicit the basic "simplifying" assumptions of
this study. The first assumption relates to the kinds of "elements"
with which any legal decision procedure can operate. The whole
of this investigation assumes that no *legislative* rules of law are
present within the legal system. That is, all the procedures analyzed are deemed to be devoid of statutes. The only kinds of legal
rules that are here considered to be available to a court are those
rules which can be or which have been made by the judiciary. The
reason for this restriction can be briefly indicated. As soon as
statutory rules of law are admitted into the decision procedures,
intricate issues of political theory become relevant. It might be
argued, for example, that a court ought always to apply the rules
of law laid down by the legislature simply because this is the
function of the judiciary in a tripartite form of government. Proper
analysis of this argument might involve considerations of the desirability of various forms of government and of the proper relations between organs of government. These are surely issues that
merit careful study, but they do not really serve the purposes of
this inquiry.

I do not mean to suggest by this that if a judiciary is furnished
with a complete code or set of legislative enactments, the problem
of how cases ought to be decided thereby disappears. Statutes are
often vague and ambiguous; unforeseen cases arise; a particular
statute may direct only that the court employ some general decision
procedure in deciding the case. If any of these or related considerations are present, then many of the issues discussed in connection
with the statute-free legal system reappear in analogous if not

identical form. Nevertheless, in cases in which the statute is precise and the relevance to the instant case relatively apparent, it can be argued that there is a justification founded upon principles of legislative supremacy or on the doctrine of the separation of powers that would require the court to decide the case in accordance with the requirements of the statute. It is this justification which I do not intend to examine and which is not readily applicable to the kind of judicial system I choose to discuss, namely, one that could be authorized either explicitly or by custom to formulate, as well as to apply, legal rules. (At appropriate times, however, I will attempt to justify on other grounds the exclusion of legislation from this study.)

A second assumption—or set of assumptions—of this study concerns the existence of certain issues that are surely relevant to the discussion and that I treat only indirectly in the body of this work. It has been suggested, for example, that it is a mistake to concentrate too heavily upon the functioning of the courts in any analysis of how conflicts are resolved by the legal system, since many of the most significant controversies are "adjudicated" outside the courtroom. The discretion exercised by the prosecuting attorney in deciding whether or not to prosecute a criminal case, the role of the police officials in deciding whether or not to make an arrest, and the function of the probation officer may have much more to do with the disposition of most disruptions of the public peace than the more formalized judicial proceedings that attend a courtroom criminal prosecution. Similarly, the extra-judicial avenues of customary business practice and the widespread reliance upon arbitration and insurance may have much more to do with the resolution of many commercial conflicts than the traditional law of contracts which is applied by the judiciary. These and analogous problems clearly deserve careful consideration. Again, however, with a view toward retaining a manageable subject of inquiry, I have purposely excluded these problems from the main area of examination, and have, on the contrary, assumed that the kind of controversy here considered is the kind that is usually dealt with by the courts in a manner characteristic of a judicial resolution of the issues.

A third important assumption relates to the question of what general function or functions a legal system ought to fulfill. Although I endeavor in this inquiry to call into question certain theses of contemporary Anglo-American jurisprudence, I do not propose to challenge the common view that the legal system ought in some very general sense to perform an essentially *utilitarian* function.* That is, I shall suppose throughout most of this study that a desirable legal system is one that succeeds in giving maximum effect to the needs, desires, interests, and aspirations of the members of the society of which it is a part. Thus, this inquiry is concerned almost exclusively with the *relationship* between this very general goal and various possible judicial decision procedures. It is, of course, legitimate to call into question the desirability of this goal, and in one chapter I do indicate briefly the direction that such a perusal might take. I do not, however, seek to do more than this for at least two reasons. First, there is the need, already mentioned, to concentrate as carefully as possible upon a relatively precise problem or set of problems. And second, the acceptance of a utilitarian function for the legal system is, for the purposes of this study, as much a matter of convenience as commitment. That is to say, although the study is avowedly concerned with the relationship between various decision procedures and a utilitarian goal, this is so in part simply because *some* goal or function of the legal system must be presupposed if evaluation is not to occur in a contextual vacuum. To a considerable extent, the persuasiveness of many of the conclusions reached in connection with an evaluation of these procedures is independent of the particular function assumed to be desirable. Thus, although some of the arguments clearly stand

---

* It should also be noted that the term "function" is ambiguous. As a descriptive word it denotes the roles, jobs, tasks, or services which the legal system *actually performs* in society. As a prescriptive term, it denotes the roles, jobs, tasks, or services which the legal system *ought to render* for society. When I speak of the function of the legal system as that of maximizing satisfactions, I am using the term prescriptively. That is, I am assuming only that this is what the legal system ought to do.

Along these same lines, it should be evident that I employ the term "normative" to mean solely "having relation to what is valuable." I do not use it to refer to the standards which may at any given time happen to exist.

or fall with the acceptance or rejection of a legal utilitarianism, others are logically independent of it.

It should be added that this utilitarian principle is deliberately stated in very general terms; and although there are many complex problems and ambiguities latent in such typically vague characterizations of utilitarianism, they can, for the most part, be safely circumvented in this inquiry.

2

The Possibility of a Deductive Procedure

A Clarification of Some Problems

In this chapter several empirical theses about the nature of legal decision procedures are considered. As noted, this study is essentially normative in purpose; it is an attempt to delineate and evaluate possible legal decision procedures. So it may therefore seem strange to begin by considering questions that are to a considerable extent descriptive in import. The oddity, however, is more apparent than real, because the claims here considered raise problems that must be dealt with by anyone who would seek to engage in normative analysis of the legal process. For these claims are often more than descriptive; most of them insist that something either must or cannot be the case.

Some legal philosophers, for example, have suggested that a case-law system such as that of England or the United States *cannot* employ rules of law* as the means by which to decide particular cases. For the unique nature of the facts of any specific case, coupled with a demonstrable nonexistence of antecedent rules of law, is believed to make it impossible for cases to be decided by appealing to such rules.

If this claim is valid, then considerable doubt is cast upon the utility of a normative study of any decision procedure which seeks to employ rules of law. In particular, since rules seem, a priori, to

---

* By rules of law I mean in general the kind of proposition that might take the form: "Either member of a partnership is liable for the entire debt of the partnership." My use of the terms "legal rule," "law," and "the law" is discussed below, pp. 36–37.

be so central to the doctrine of precedent, the fruitfulness of a study of that procedure is sure to be in question from the outset. This is not, of course, to suggest that normative inquiry is useless whenever an evaluation of anything but the given state of affairs is undertaken. Questions of what *ought to be* have relevance and meaning quite apart from the question of what *is*. But the claim about facts and legal rules has a considerably stronger implication, for it insists that a rule-applying procedure cannot be realized or put into practice. Perhaps an analysis of a decision procedure that employed rules would still have merit as an ideal by which to evaluate actual systems. Nevertheless a procedure which *could not* be put into operation under any circumstances has appreciably less significance, even as an ideal, than one which could be so employed. That the domain of the potential is more extensive than the domain of the actual is clear; that the realm of the desirable is not included within the limits of the potential is less certain. On this ground alone it would be necessary to consider such claims prior to any evaluation of different judicial decision procedures. But there are additional reasons for beginning with non-normative theses. The writers who are here considered have purported to concern themselves almost entirely with descriptive analysis. Consequently, considerations of expository fairness require that this orientation be unaltered. It should be observed, however, that although certain views are presented here as essentially empirical, and although their authors have insisted that empirical questions are their chief concern, no such careful distinction is preserved in the writings themselves. Indeed, the consistent use of imprecise terminology makes it very difficult to determine, among other things, precisely where description has ended and prescription has begun.

There is a real sense in which much of what is suggested in this study may be neither novel nor unanticipated. I have sought throughout to clarify what I regard as ambiguous claims about the legal decision process and its constituents. It may well be that my conclusions are no different from those which philosophers have been suggesting (at least implicitly) all the time. On the other hand, the ambiguity with which many legal philosophers have stated their positions makes it equally possible to understand them to have made radically different proposals. By beginning with an exposition of these various philosophical views, it is easier to point up the places at which equivocal explication and argumentation require clarification and the exploration of alternative interpretations. For example, as previously noted, the characteristics of a deductive or logical decision procedure have been criticized far more often than they have been elucidated. Thus, the various elements that might be thought to constitute or to be implied by a "deductive" decision procedure must be delineated before either this procedure or its alternatives can be evaluated.

THE DEDUCTIVE THEORY AND ITS CRITICS

The question of the nature of the judicial decision process has been formulated by almost every legal philosopher as involving the issue of whether or not courts reach their decisions by a deductive or logical method of decision. Many legal philosophers have come to regard the deductive theory, i.e., the theory that is thought to describe (or propose) an essentially deductive or logical judicial decision procedure, as the chief impediment to clear and consistent thinking about the judicial process. Critics of the theory have given it a variety of names. It has been called "legal fundamentalism," "formalism," "deductivism," "the phonographic theory of law," "mechanical jurisprudence," "slot machine jurisprudence," and a host of comparable epithets.[1] Yet, the proliferation of labels has not been accompanied by a clarification of the characteristics of the procedure or the reasons for its rejection. Indeed, as we have noted, the general attack upon the use of logic in the judicial decision process resolves itself into one or more of a variety of claims and suppositions.

What, for example, would a deductive decision procedure be like? What does the deductive theory entail? Many critics have

---

[1] Superscript numbers refer to the Notes at the back of the book, pp. 177–88. Except for some explanatory remarks which appear at the foot of the page, all direct citations and discursive commentary will be found in the Notes.

thought the deductive theory to imply a judicial decision procedure in which all cases are decided by an appeal to rules that are certain and unchanging, whose application is completely predictable. It is regarded as in some sense postulating "a gapless system of pre-existing law, from which a solution for every new case could be obtained by deduction."[2] In such a system, apparently, the rule of law relevant to the case serves as the major premise of a syllogism; the statement that characterizes the particular fact situation before the court serves as the minor premise; and that conclusion which is derivable in accordance with the canons of Aristotelian logic is announced by the judge as the court's decision for this particular case. It would seem that the judge is peculiarly qualified to render decisions because he knows what many of the rules are, where the others may be readily located, and how to use the canons of logic to discern valid arguments.

Critics of the deductive theory also suggest that the theory necessarily denies the relevance of considerations of justice to the selection of the propositions that serve as the major and minor premises and to the conclusion that becomes the decision for the particular case.[3] Concomitantly, since the judge's sole function is to apply the existing rules of law to the facts of the particular case, the deductive theory is deemed to entail the view that it is never the province of the judge to make rules of law. Thus when philosophers pronounce the deductive theory unacceptable, they attack, among other things, a procedure in which rules of law could never be formulated or altered by the judge, a procedure in which the judge plays no "creative" role in the decision process, a procedure that finds relevant the canons of formal logic, and a procedure in which there is seemingly no guarantee that justice will be done in all or even most cases. If the deductive theory, so interpreted, correctly describes even some of the characteristics of the English or American legal system, it surely furnishes the grounds for a harsh indictment of the way English or American courts have decided cases.

In developing their criticism, opponents of the deductive theory have almost unanimously regarded the words of Justice Holmes as the most appropriate single point of departure for their attack.

The dictum that "general propositions do not decide concrete cases" and the assertion that "the life of the law has not been logic: it has been experience,"[4] have been taken to signify that rules of law were not the means by which courts decided particular cases. These aphorisms have been understood at times to suggest that a logical application of rules to facts cannot have been the procedure by which adjudication actually was effected. And they have been interpreted, too, as a demand for an analysis that will realistically—and hence, accurately—study the decision process of the common-law courts.

When such an analysis is undertaken, the critics insist, one readily discovers that courts have in fact responded to novel situations and changing pressures. And how, it is asked, "is it possible for courts by supposedly necessary logical deduction from noncontemporaneous premises and apparently without entering upon social and ethical inquiries, to reach conclusions well adapted to contemporary problems?"[5] The answer is simple. The deductive theory is an inadequate, quite inaccurate account of the way in which courts really have decided cases. Courts both past and present have clearly not invoked a formal procedure by which particular cases are adjudicated in accordance with rules; on the contrary, their methodology has been, and continues to be, distinctively nondeductive.

The language of judicial decision is mainly the language of logic. And the logical method and form flatter that longing for certainty and for repose which is in every human mind. But certainty generally is illusion, and repose is not the destiny of man. Behind the logical form lies a judgment as to the relative worth and importance of competing legislative grounds, often an inarticulate and unconscious judgment, it is true, and yet the very root and nerve of the whole proceeding.[6]

Why then has it taken so long to see the weaknesses of the deductive theory? Why, since common-law courts have been deciding cases for over 750 years, did the theory's inaccuracy remain hidden until the twentieth century? Again, the answer is soon found. If one were to look no further than the opinions that judges write to accompany their decisions, it would not occur to one that the decision process could be anything but deductive. For it is one of the curious features of Anglo-American case law that regardless of the way in which a given decision is actually reached, the judge apparently feels it necessary to make it appear that the decision was dictated by prior rules applied in accordance with canons of formal logic.[7] One thing must be added, however. It would be incorrect to ascribe to the judiciary sinister motives of any kind. Judges do not deliberately seek to deceive the world about the nature of the decision process. The fact that their opinions obscure rather than illuminate the judicial process indicates that the departure from the deductive model is effected quite unconsciously.[8]

That the courts have in fact—but not in their opinions—used a nondeductive, non-rule-applying decision procedure is an empirical premise which, it is asserted, may be substantiated by careful analysis of what was actually done in particular cases. Those who are critical of the deductive theory have filled the literature with numerous examples. The way in which the United States Supreme Court interpreted the Sherman Act is, Jerome Frank suggests, a case in point. Until 1911 the court consistently refused to construe this statute as applying only to unreasonable restraints of trade. In the *Standard Oil* and *Tobacco* cases,[9] however, both decided in 1911, the court obviously reversed itself and held that the statute did apply solely to unreasonable restraints. What is of interest here, Frank insists, is not the fact that the court changed its mind but rather that Judge White, speaking for the court, "went to elaborate care to avoid admitting that the law could be modified by the courts and was therefore possibly unconstant and unpredictable."[10]

Similarly, according to Julius Stone the "legal category of concealed circuitous reference" is an example of the type of argumentation invoked by the courts in such a manner that the real nature of the decision procedure is obscured.[11] In *Donoghue v. Stevenson*,[12] the court was confronted with a tort case involving duty and negligence. It formulated a criterion for determining whether a duty relationship is present. We owe a duty, the court said, to those who are in the position of "neighbors" to us. Neighbors, moreover, are those "who are so closely and directly affected by my act that I ought reasonably to have them in contemplation as being so affected when I am directing my mind to the acts or omissions which are called into question." But this formulation of the duty relationship, Stone argues, is one aspect of what is usually thought of as the test for negligence. It would seem therefore that to the extent to which duty is supposed by the courts to be a pre-requisite to the question of negligence, the two issues are in fact identical. From this it may be inferred that "if the 'duty' require-ment is merely tautologous with the 'negligence' requirement, and if courts do nevertheless still purport to relieve some defend-ants of the consequences of 'negligence' by holding that there is no duty, it must be obvious again *that there is some determinant of the actual decision other than can be drawn by deductive logic from the category ostensibly used.*"[13]

The arguments against the deductive theory do not terminate with the presentation of examples of the presence of nondeductive procedures. For it has been insisted as well that the deductive theory cannot take account of three necessary features of a non-statutory system. The first feature relates to the question of what are to be regarded as *the facts* of a case. It is a necessary precon-dition of the deductive theory, some argue, that courts can only apply the rules of prior cases to a fact situation that is identical to the situation of the earlier case or cases. Even if it is assumed that a rule of law is enunciated by a prior case, that rule is only applicable to a subsequent situation identical to the earlier case. But if it is admitted that this is a necessary condition of the de-ductive theory, then the process cannot describe the way in which legal controversies are adjudicated by the judge. For it is quite evident that no two cases are ever alike in all details. At a very minimum, the time and place of the controversy are always dif-ferent. Consequently, it follows that a judge cannot be "bound" by prior cases because there cannot be prior cases that are identical to the instant case. From this it may be inferred that some pro-cedure which does not require an identity relationship between two or more cases must have been employed.

If this objection is not conclusive, there is another one related to it that surely is; this objection concerns the problems that at-tend the classifying of any concrete case as a case of a particular kind. For even if it is assumed that there are relatively precise rules of law which the judge can apply, these can only be so applied once the case has been characterized as being a member of the class controlled by a given rule. Thus, the decision reached in any particular case will depend not upon the particular rules of the legal system but rather upon the characterization which the judge makes of the particular fact situation. And, once more, since this process of characterization is not a logical or deductive procedure, it follows that the judge can characterize the fact situation any way he wishes in order to produce the desired result.[14]

An analogous argument has been offered to demonstrate that a comparable problem arises whenever an attempt is made to determine the rule of law enunciated by a case. According to the deductive theory—and, indeed, to case-law theory in general—the only "binding" aspect of a case is the *ratio decidendi*. "Any judgment of any court is authoritative only as to that part of it, called the *ratio decidendi*, which is considered to have been necessary to the decision of the actual issue between the litigants."[15] The rules of law that according to the deductive theory the courts have applied are, therefore, only those rules that were necessary to decide the particular cases.

The descriptive inadequacy of the deductive theory now becomes obvious. For, as has been insisted, it is evident that we can derive "a parallel series of corresponding propositions of law, each more and more generalized as we recede farther and farther from the instant state of facts and include more and more fact situations in the successive groupings."[16] As a consequence, the supposed effect of the *ratio decidendi* is necessarily illusory. Any rule of law can be derived from the holding and opinion of the prior case, and this rule is as properly the *ratio decidendi* as is any other rule. The earlier case can have only the meaning that the judge in the later case wants it to have. In a real sense, then, the rules of law which "dictate" the decisions in particular cases have of necessity existed only after the fact of decision in the particular case. The rule of law which necessarily controls any fact situation can never exist, that is, until after that fact situation has been adjudicated. The choice by the judge of what shall be the rule for this case and the decision concerning how the case is to be characterized are the real features in the decision process. And neither problem can be solved by the use of logic or deduction.

It is, then, this analysis of what the courts in fact do and this delineation of the character of the materials with which judges inevitably work that have led to the rejection of the deductive theory of legal reasoning as a correct description of the judicial decision process. For the most part, discussion has ceased at this point. Alternative expositions have been hinted at but not developed. To the extent to which positive descriptions of the nature of the decision process have been suggested, at least three might be mentioned.

But first of all it should be made clear that the extremely brief summaries that follow are not offered for the purpose of disputing their correctness as descriptive generalizations. Rather, they are presented solely in order to indicate some of the kinds of answers that have been given to the question: "If courts have not used rules to decide cases, what have they used?" As will be shown below, both the rejection of the deductive theory and the acceptance of any one or all of the three following descriptions rest in large part upon a serious oversimplification of the question just posed.*

It has been suggested by some that a hunch or intuition of what is the just solution for the particular case is the crucial factor in the decision process.[17] If one is to have an accurate understanding of the process of decision employed by the courts, one must ignore the opinions that judges have written and concentrate instead upon the actual results reached in concrete cases. And there one finds "that courts are dominantly coerced, not by the essays of their predecessors but by a surer thing—*by an intuition of fitness of solution to problem.*"[18] The opinions that talk of the application of a rule to the facts of the case are systematically misleading accounts

---

* There is a further reason for presenting these theories in capsule form at this time. Although they are treated here as purely *descriptive* in character, it is not clear that this is all their authors intended them to be. Indeed, as initially presented, they contain strong prescriptive implication as well. An analysis of this aspect is reserved, however, for Chapter 5, where these theories will receive more careful attention.

of the way in which cases are really decided, because the real process of decision is intuitive and not deductive.

The view that the judicial decision process is not a distinctively logical one is shared, as we have seen, by Jerome Frank. He, too, insists that the judge usually begins with the conclusion that he deems proper and only later seeks to rationalize this result by purporting to show that it derives necessarily from the "relevant" legal rule. Frank does not, however, isolate the hunch or intuition of justice as the determinative factor in judicial decisions. Rather, the decision process that was in fact employed in any particular case can, he urges, be correctly described only by reference to the "peculiarly individual traits of the persons whose inferences and opinions are to be explained."[19] In short, the *personality* of the judge is the key to an understanding of the way in which cases have been decided.

Still a third view of the judicial decision process holds that the judge's emotional reaction to the facts of the case is what has really determined the outcome reached.[20] Once again the rules of law referred to in judicial opinions are not the criteria by which cases are decided. Rather, they are the linguistic vehicle by which the judge has revealed his preference for a particular decision. If a judge desires that one set of legal consequences should affect the parties, he announces a legal rule that will bring these consequences about; if he desires a contrary rule, a different rule is pronounced. In short, rules of law are nothing more than expressions of the judge's desire.[21] And it is his desires or preferences that really have decided cases.

To recapitulate: Beginning with the premise that the courts of the Anglo-American legal system have responded to the needs and desires of the community, it has been inferred that the deductive theory for this reason necessarily cannot be a correct description of the decision procedure that has in fact been used by the courts in their adjudication of particular cases. Furthermore, the deductive theory is necessarily an incorrect account of the decision process of a nonstatutory legal system because it fails: (a) to take account of the fact that no two cases can ever be identical; (b) to realize that the operation of characterization is a crucial but non-deductive procedure; and (c) to recognize that there cannot be *antecedent* legal rules binding on the judge. Finally, three alternative descriptions of the decision process have been suggested: one holding that intuition is the procedure by which the judge decides a case, another that his personality is determinative, and a third that he decides according to his emotions or preferences.

SOME CRITICISMS OF THE CRITICS

The preceding exposition of the views held by the critics of the deductive theory succeeds in indicating some of the confusions that pervade the discussion of the role of logic in the law. Before it can be decided whether the courts have employed, or could or should employ, a deductive decision procedure, it is important that the issues involved be delineated with greater clarity.

As we have noted, critics of the deductive theory have, among other things, sought to call attention to the fact that the rules of syllogistic validity and invalidity cannot be employed in any obvious sense to evaluate the content of either premises or conclusions. It would, therefore, seem to follow that any theory of the legal decision process which described it as a wholly syllogistic procedure would at best be incomplete simply because the theory would necessarily fail to describe the way in which the premises were to be selected. At the same time, many legal philosophers also attribute to the deductive theory the thesis that the rules of law which are to serve as the major premises of the syllogism must be pre-existent and unchanging. And here, they insist, the deductive theory is not merely incomplete; it is incorrect.

Now, it is not within the scope of this inquiry to discuss the question of whether the courts of England or the United States ever adhered to a decision procedure based solely upon precedent. It is, however, relevant to ask whether courts could have done so if they wished. It is even more relevant (for our purposes) to decide whether they should employ this decision procedure. Both these questions are considered later. But what should be noted here is the lack of any necessary connection between a procedure that uses the canons of formal logic to assess certain relationships between premises and conclusions and a procedure that derives all its premises from a body of already formulated and articulated legal rules. It may indeed be true that the syllogism can neither furnish nor evaluate the content of propositions, but it does not follow that a procedure which seeks to use the syllogism to "test" the validity of arguments is thereby committed to employ any particular method for deriving the premises of these arguments. Courts cannot have used the syllogism to decide which premises to select; but this by itself does not show that they did not use the syllogism as a means for assessing the validity of arguments they formulated; this by itself does not show that the courts necessarily relied upon a body of pre-existing laws as the source for their premises.

Many philosophers would agree, no doubt, that so far the deductive theory has only been shown to be incomplete. They would be quick to add, though, that the deductive theory (when so limited) now ceases to be an interesting description of how cases are decided. For, they would insist, if a theory does not tell how rules of law are to be selected to serve as major premises or how minor premises are to be "derived" from fact situations, it omits a description of almost all the factors that are really determinative in the judicial decision process. It may or may not be true that courts employed the canons of formal logic once they had formulated their syllogisms, but since they did not, and in fact could not, have used these rules to derive their premises, the deductive theory at best serves to focus attention upon subsidiary rather than central considerations.

If the above argument constituted the major objection to the accuracy of the deductive theory, it would be relatively innocuous. But many of the critics of the deductive theory who talk most disparagingly about the possibility of a logical decision procedure have apparently sought to make a much stronger point. And they have done so, I submit, only by making the kind of mistake that pervades so many discussions of the place of logic in the law. The mistake, here termed the *irrationalist fallacy*, consists in this: The question of whether an argument is formally valid is confused with the question of whether there can be good reasons for believing a proposition to be true or false. It is recognized quite correctly that the canons of formal logic have a decidedly limited applicability. It is inferred quite incorrectly from this that all the questions which cannot be settled by appealing to formal logic cannot be settled in any manner which could be called "reasonable" or "logical." An appeal to formal logic is equated with an appeal to criteria of rationality or reasonableness, and it is concluded that because the courts cannot have used formal logic to select or formulate legal premises, the courts cannot have appealed to any rational or objective criteria when engaged in these undertakings. Perhaps the philosophers who insist so vehemently that the deductive theory is hopelessly wrong are not wholly serious on this point, but they do say that most of the important problems which arise in the decision of cases must be settled by the court in an arbitrary fashion *because* they cannot be settled by appealing to the canons of Aristotelian logic.[22] It is one thing, however, to contrast a logical or deductive decision procedure with a procedure in which good or persuasive reasons are the best that can be required; it is something quite different to oppose the criteria of logic or rationalism to those of feeling, emotion, sensory experience, or unanalyzed personal predilection.[23]

I am not suggesting here that the deductive theory should be interpreted as the theory which describes the courts as having given good reasons for the selection of their premises. Nor am I proposing that as a matter of fact there were or are objective criteria to which the courts have appealed in resolving the kinds of problems that could not be resolved by invoking the aid of the syllogism. Nor, for that matter, am I implying that the talk about "giving good reasons" or "appealing to objective criteria" is itself free from imprecision. I am arguing only that many legal philosophers are surely mistaken if they infer the inherent arbitrariness of the judicial decision process from the limited utility of formal, deductive logic. It may not make much sense to describe the judicial decision process as a completely deductive one. But it makes even less sense to insist that for this reason courts could not (and should not) employ a procedure or set of procedures that permits of some kind of reasoned justification for the judicial decisions reached by those courts.

At the beginning of this chapter it was observed that the question "What is the nature of the judicial decision process?" might be ambiguous, since it is not clear whether a descriptive or a prescriptive reply is being requested, nor whether this is a demand for a single monolithic response that must adequately describe all decisions, or only a request for an answer that can account for the most important or significant ones. In the light of the foregoing discussion it is necessary to ask whether there may not be still a third kind of ambiguity contained within or implied by the question. For the phrase "judicial decision process" is, I submit, capable in itself of denoting two quite different procedures, neither of which has as yet been carefully isolated or described. And until this is done, intelligent inquiry into the nature of the judicial decision process cannot be effected, nor can the issue of the correctness of the deductive theory be resolved.

Placing the problem within the broader context of decision procedures in general, there are two quite distinctive procedures that might be followed before any particular decision is made or accepted. This is as true in science or ethics as it is in law. The way in which these two procedures operate can be indicated by reference to two types of questions that may be asked about any decision. One kind of question asks about the manner in which a decision or conclusion was reached; the other inquires whether a given decision or conclusion is justifiable. That is to say, a person who examines a decision process may want to know about the factors that led to or produced the conclusion; he may also be interested in the manner in which the conclusion was to be justified.

Consider the following three examples:

(1) I see a person helping a blind man across the street and I ask him why he aided the blind man. The person might reply: "I helped him because I thought he would give me a tip."

(2) A scientist who has discovered a vaccine which purportedly provides complete immunization against cancer informs the scientific community that he hit upon this particular chemical combination in the following manner. He wrote down 1,000 possible chemical combinations on separate pieces of paper, put them all into a big hat, and pulled out one of the pieces at random.

(3) Charles A. Beard reports that the drafters of the Constitu-

tion were members of the propertied class who desired to per-
petuate many of their own class values within the framework of
the new government.[24]

Now, all three of these examples tell something about how a
particular conclusion or decision was reached. None of these examples, it can be argued, answers the question of whether any
one of these conclusions is in any sense a justified or justifiable
conclusion.

In the first example it might be argued that the answer given
is irrelevant to the question of whether the action of helping a
blind man to cross a street (the decision or conclusion) is a
morally desirable act. For both parties might agree that the expectation of a reward does not constitute a morally good reason
for behaving in a specified manner.

The second example makes the point still clearer. The scientist has announced how he arrived at the conclusion that this chemical formula might immunize against cancer, but of course he has
not answered the question of whether the vaccine will in fact immunize. How the scientist happened to select the formula is one
question. Whether this formula is an effective vaccine, whether
the conclusion can be empirically validated, is quite a different one.
Furthermore, if *ex hypothesi* the vaccine were effective, it would
certainly not be rejected because of the way in which the scientist
selected it for testing.

In the same manner and for the same reasons, it may be observed that a knowledge of the motives of the drafters of the Constitution does not answer the question of whether the Constitution establishes a desirable or justifiable form of government.
Evaluation of the worth of the Constitution can, it would seem,
be conducted quite independently of an awareness of the motives
of the Founding Fathers.

The above three examples, therefore, tend to explain the way
in which a conclusion was reached. In certain contexts they do
not respond to the question of whether the conclusion is in fact
justifiable. Just as these two kinds of questions can be roughly
distinguished, so the factors that led to the "discovery" of the conclusion can be differentiated from the process by which it is to be

justified. I will refer to the procedure by which a conclusion is reached as the *process of discovery*, and to the procedure by which a conclusion is justified as the *process of justification.*

Having succeeded in establishing a rigid dichotomy between these two procedures, we must indicate three ways in which they may be related in actual practice. In the first place it should be evident that there is nothing immutable about any particular process of discovery or justification. Various procedures of discovery are possible; so too are various processes of justification. In both instances the procedure may be highly ordered or formalized, or it may be quite unsystematic and haphazard. When the procedure has a regular pattern that is systematically employed in each instance of discovery or justification, it might be called a "logic of discovery" or a "logic of justification," the word logic denoting precisely that attribute of order of procedure.

In the second place, for any given conjunction of a process of discovery and a process of justification an asymmetrical relationship obtains between them. That is to say, a procedure of discovery may be adopted if it succeeds in "generating" more conclusions that can be justified within the accepted logic of justification than any other discovery procedure. In a real sense the logic of justification provides the criteria by which both particular conclusions and the procedures of discovery may be evaluated; it is not easy to see how the converse could be true for any logic of discovery.

And finally, it would be a mistake to conclude that because two separable procedures are involved, they are not usually performed by the same individual. Indeed, although it is not always true, it is generally assumed that one should not put forward a conclusion or act upon a decision until one has subjected it to, and substantiated it by, one's logic of justification. This is perhaps what is meant by *rational behavior.*

I have labored this point both because it is one that is seldom appreciated by legal philosophers and because it is directly relevant to many of the theories that concern themselves with the nature of legal reasoning. For if someone talks about the legal decision process, he might be seeking to ask the kinds of questions that are relevant to an understanding of what I have called the process of discovery. But he might also be endeavoring to pose questions which relate to the procedure of justification that was employed. I think that at least some of the legal philosophers discussed above have tended to ask plausible questions about discovery. Those who have stressed the inadequacies of the deductive theory and who have sought to substitute some other description in its place have perhaps shed much light upon the discovery procedures used by the courts. By equating the process of discovery with the process of decision they have argued quite persuasively that the judge's *opinion* is surely not an accurate report of the decision process. And indeed, if the decision process is coextensive with the process of discovery, it is probable that they are correct.[25]

But it is, I think, chimerical to suppose that most judicial opinions purport to describe the process of discovery. Surely the kind of reasoning process that is evidenced by the usual judicial opinion is more suggestive of a typical justificatory procedure. Turning by way of analogy to the example of the scientist—it is one thing to read a judicial opinion as a report of why or how the judge "hit upon" the decision and quite another thing to read the opinion as an account of the procedure he employed in "testing" it. To insist—as many legal philosophers appear to have done—that a judicial opinion is an accurate description of the decision process there employed if and only if it faithfully describes the procedure of discovery is to help to *guarantee* that the opinion will be found wanting. But if the opinion is construed to be a report of the justificatory procedure employed by the judge, then the not infrequent reliance upon such things as rules of law and rules of logic seems more plausible. For conceivably, at least, some judges have felt that before they render a decision in a case they must be able to justify that decision. They may have had a hunch that a particular decision would be "right," they may have had a grudge against a particular defendant or plaintiff, but they might also have felt that considerations of this kind do not count as justifications for rendering a binding judicial decision, and that unless they could justify the decision "they would like to give" by appealing to certain other criteria, the decision ought not to be handed down as binding upon the litigants. And it may just be that some judges have thought they must be able to establish a formally valid relationship between the decision and certain more general premises, and able also to give good reasons for the premises so selected. If this is so, then the attacks upon the deductive theory are not wrong; they are simply irrelevant.

It is sometimes urged that simply because courts use a deductive procedure as a procedure of justification, the adherence to such a procedure must be an ineffectual means of restricting the kinds of decisions that courts can appropriately render. As is so often true, it is very difficult to tell exactly what the objection is or how to refute it. Jerome Frank, for example, seems hopelessly equivocal on this point. He asserts, and I think wholly correctly, that there is a sense in which judging of all kinds begins "with a conclusion more or less vaguely formed; a man ordinarily starts with such a conclusion and afterwards tries to find premises which will substantiate it. If he cannot, to his satisfaction, find proper arguments, . . . he will, unless he is arbitrary or mad, reject the conclusion and seek another." This is roughly what I mean by *justification.* But then Frank goes on to say just as emphatically that "There is no rule by which you can force a judge to follow an old rule or by which you can predict when he will verbalize his conclusion in the form of a new rule, or by which he can determine when to consider a case as an exception to an old rule, or by which he can make up his mind whether to select one or another old rule to explain or guide his judgment. His decision is primary, the rules he may happen to refer to are incidental."[26]

Now, it is surely difficult to reconcile these two passages. In the first one Frank implies quite strongly that there are or might be criteria which would force a person to reject a conclusion which had been tentatively formed. Yet, in the second he insists that there is no explanation which a judge could give for having appealed to one rule rather than to another as the justification for his decision. Again, a few pages later Frank says, "We have seen that one of their [legal rules' and principles'] chief uses is to enable the judges to give formal justifications—rationalizations—of the conclusions at which they otherwise arrive." Here, as elsewhere, Frank appears to equate the process of justification with the process of rationalization. But surely, as he himself has admitted, these need not be the same. In fact, on the very next page, he observes that "the conscientious judge, having tentatively arrived at a conclusion, can check up to see whether such a conclusion, without unfair distortion of the facts, can be linked with the generalized points of view theretofore acceptable. If none such are discoverable, he is forced to consider more acutely whether his tentative conclusion is wise, both with respect to the case before him and with respect to possible implications for future cases."[27]

Frank sometimes seems to be saying that all justification is necessarily rationalization (in the currently accepted connotation of the term), that a reason can always be given for a conclusion, and that therefore the requirement that judges justify their decisions can never have any effect upon the decisions they will render. Just as often, however, he appears to be suggesting that judges have not tried to justify their decisions very conscientiously, that they have been content with mere rationalizations, and that they ought to adhere to stricter canons of justification which are, apparently, capable of formulation.

These are, however, two dramatically different theses, and they must be kept distinct. If justifications are necessarily mere rationalizations, then there is little utility in worrying about the kinds of justifications which ought to be required. But if the acceptance of criteria of justification could make a difference in the decisions which a court would render, then the specification and evaluation of alternative criteria is a significant undertaking.

It is important that the points at issue be clear. Since this work is concerned primarily with a normative rather than an empirical analysis, I do not wish to insist that the courts of any legal system have as a matter of fact universally employed any particular justificatory procedure. Indeed, it would be amazing if any one procedure had been used in all cases. And as we will notice later, there is rather conclusive evidence that different courts have invoked quite different procedures. It should also be made clear that I do not want to maintain that courts should employ as their procedure of justification the kind of procedure which the opinions of some courts indicate was employed. What I do urge, however, is that the meaning of "decision process" be clarified; until it is, meaningful discussion on either a descriptive or a prescriptive level is difficult, if not impossible. I have tried to show the results of the failure to clarify it by suggesting that the proponents and the opponents of the deductive theory quite possibly have not been talking about the same procedure. If the talk about judicial hunches, emotions, and personalities relates to questions of discovery, it need not be inconsistent with a wholly different analysis concerning procedures of justification. Thus I do suggest that questions pertaining to justification can usefully be kept distinct from questions about discovery. And I propose finally that there do not seem to be any very persuasive reasons for believing that the adoption of some procedures of justification could not have an important effect upon the way in which courts decide particular cases.

But before any normative analysis of different procedures of justification is possible, it is necessary to confront the objections specified earlier concerning the impossibility of any kind of decision procedure that seeks to make legal rules relevant to the rendering of a judicial decision. For among the procedures of justification that will be considered are those which expressly stipulate that legal rules and "logic" ought to be important constituents of the apparatus of justification. Thus, the claims relating to the uniqueness of fact situations, the arbitrariness of classification, and the nonexistence of binding rules of law must be examined in order to see whether it is even useful to consider procedures of justification which are in any way "deductive" or "logical."

The objection to the importance or relevance of a deductive procedure on the grounds that no two fact situations can be the same is a most curious one. For in one sense the assertion that every fact situation is unique is both unobjectionable and unimpeachable. The mere fact that *two* fact situations are hypothesized seems sufficient to establish the claim that they are different in *some* respect. Yet, by admitting this one does not in fact concede the *necessary* inapplicability or unworkability of a rule-applying procedure. Rather, the real issue would appear to be whether this almost self-evident claim poses any special problems for the possible applicability of legal rules to fact situations. I do not see how, by itself, the claim succeeds in doing so. Surely there is a sense in which any two legal situations are different from one another, but this seems to be the same sense in which any two existential situations necessarily differ from one another. There are, admittedly, perplexing philosophical problems concerning the manner in which we are able to know that any two objects are both objects of the same kind. How do we know that two objects, for example, are both chairs, both tables, or both persons? Because they are different from one another in many respects, why are we entitled to say that each is a chair? Or a table? Or a person? What justifies picking out or emphasizing certain characteristics they have in common rather than the characteristics which make them distinguishable? These are, it should be repeated, important and difficult questions. But unless it can be shown that there is something special about legal "objects," i.e., the components of the fact situations with which courts must concern themselves, it is not clear that the mere insistence upon the "uniqueness" of objects *qua* objects poses special problems for the legal system. It would seem, on the contrary, that without attempting to solve these philosophical problems, two fact situations could be classified by a court as being of the same kind for precisely the same reasons or on exactly the same grounds that two material objects may both be correctly called "chairs," "tables," or "persons."

But, as noted earlier, this objection is closely related to another one that is more relevant to peculiarly legal problems. The argument is that since the real issue is one of characterizing or classifying particular fact situations, and since this is necessarily a nondeductive procedure, the emphasis upon logic in the law can serve only to focus attention upon the subsidiary rather than the central aspects of the legal decision process.

It should once again be conceded that there is clearly a sense in which the activity of characterization cannot be governed by the rules of formal or deductive logic. This is so for at least two reasons. First, it is surely correct to observe that "fact situations do not await us neatly labeled, creased, and folded, nor is their legal classification written on them to be simply read off by the judge." And second, even if this were not the case, it would still be true that "logic does not prescribe interpretation of terms; it dictates neither the stupid nor intelligent interpretation of any expression."[28] One cannot appeal to the canons of logic to decide whether a given classification is necessarily the correct one.

If this alone were the thrust of the objection, it would be unassailable. But as we have seen, those who have talked about the problem of classification have often seemed to make a stronger point: namely, that because classification cannot be carried on deductively, the task of classification is an inherently arbitrary one. Because the rules of logic are irrelevant at this juncture, it is thought that there cannot be objective criteria to which appeal can be made. The judge, this argument seems to imply, can choose to regard any fact or type of fact as determining the classification selected and by this means reach or justify any conclusion he desires.

This argument raises several points. To begin with a trivial one, it is probably correct that the judge *can* select any factors he wishes as determining the characterization of the fact situation. If this is a proposition about the actual, physical capabilities of the judge, it is sufficiently irrelevant to be dismissed at once.

A more plausible interpretation of this thesis would construe it as asserting that there are no *grounds* upon which a given characterization may be criticized—in other words, that there is no sense in which a particular classification could be termed "correct" or "incorrect," "reasonable" or "unreasonable." Once again, it would seem that critics of the deductive theory have committed the irrationalist fallacy. They have mistakenly inferred that a logical (in the broad sense of a "well-reasoned") argument for a classification cannot be given because logic (in the technical sense of Aristotelian or formal logic) cannot be used to characterize fact situations. The important question, which this inference obscures, is whether it can make sense to ask the judge to justify the way in which he has characterized a given case.

One argument for the proposition that this question is a meaningful one takes the following form: There are some or perhaps many fact situations which so obviously can be characterized (for legal purposes) in one and only one fashion that any other characterization would immediately be perceived to be erroneous or arbitrary. The case may be such a "perfect" instance of what is designated by the "standard" or "settled" usage of a legal term that no question of its classification can reasonably arise within the context of the case before the court.[29]

There are many who might accept an argument of this kind, but who would add that there are also cases which do pose a real problem of classification. There are, to use H. L. A. Hart's term, "penumbral cases" on which settled usage is silent and for which alternative classifications appear reasonable. Here, "someone must take the responsibility of deciding that words do or do not cover some case in hand with all the practical consequences involved in this decision." It is entirely possible that those who have attacked "deductivism" have sought to call attention to the existence and importance of "penumbral cases." But, once more, it is not very clear what is thought to follow from the recognition that cases of this kind do arise. Does this imply only that "standard usage" cannot be the criterion for the classification of any cases? Does it mean as well that no criteria can be formulated? Or does it mean that the criteria which could be formulated will necessarily permit of alternative "reasonable" classifications?[30]

To a very great extent, all of these possible implications rest upon the view that a distinction can be made between common and novel cases. This is a position which is examined later in the inquiry (in particular in Chapters 5 and 7). As will be suggested, a convincing case can perhaps be made for the view that the same kinds of criteria which can be used to evaluate legal rules can also be used to justify classification of facts. That is to say, it will be proposed that the question of which characteristics shall be regarded as "legally" significant is another form of the question of what kinds of legal rules are desirable. For the present it is sufficient to observe that even if standard usage cannot or should not be the criterion for novel cases, and even if, therefore, an important decision concerning classification must be made in at least these cases, it does not necessarily follow—if anyone has thought it does—that the decision is for this reason an inherently arbitrary one.

Many of the same arguments, *mutatis mutandis*, can be applied to objections such as Oliphant's concerning the determination of the legal rule. Once again it must be readily admitted that a judge *can* extract a *ratio decidendi* of almost any order of generality from a particular case. But once more it must also be insisted that the real question is different in import, namely, are there criteria by which this process of rule-determination can in general be governed? Surely it is often the case that a later judge does determine what is "holding" and what is "dictum." But why does this imply that the choice need be arbitrary or unlimited?

There is, moreover, a further point that can be made in the discussion of legal rules. Even if it is conceded that the criteria by which the *rule* of a case is to be determined must always be vague and imprecise, it is nevertheless often true that an explicit formulation of a legal rule can be found in a court's opinion. And despite the fact that so many authors vehemently insist that the *opinion* is *never* binding upon other courts,[31] it would appear that many times it is precisely the rule enunciated in the *opinion* which has been held to be controlling later cases. It is more than a little surprising that those who are the most insistent upon seeing what the courts *really* do, also insist that judges never accept the rule which is stated in the opinion of some prior case.

The Anglo-American legal system proliferates in examples of precisely this kind of judicial activity. One such example looms large in the law of contract remedies. In the opinion in the case of *Hadley v. Baxendale*,[32] Baron Anderson laid down a rule by which damages for breach of contract were to be measured in certain types of situations. This rule has been followed almost without exception in many jurisdictions.[33] What is really interesting about the rule, however, is not so much the fact that it was articulated in the opinion and has been followed by other courts, but that it can be argued that the rule as formulated was incorrectly applied to the facts in *Hadley v. Baxendale*.[34] Now, if the "rule" of a case were always the holding and never the opinion, then it would seem that the holding in *Hadley v. Baxendale* (which is demonstrably inconsistent with the rule in the opinion) should have been followed by later courts. But this is not so; it is the rule stated in the opinion that has been followed.[35] Thus, often the courts do not need criteria to determine the "rule" of a case, simply because they accept the rule as it is formulated in the opinion.

Once again, the relevance of these observations should perhaps be stressed. This is not to insist upon the desirability of a procedure in which the rules explicitly laid down in prior cases are inexorably followed in later cases. The remainder of this study is devoted to this very question. The description here presented is offered only in order to refute the claim that rules of law of this form cannot be operative within a legal system devoid of statutes; as we have seen, they have in fact been operative.

The recognition of the fact that courts have laid down rules of law that have been followed in subsequent cases provides a convenient point of departure for discussion of a final issue that must be dealt with at the outset of this study. There are few questions, if any, to which legal philosophers have devoted more attention than "the nature of law." It is impossible to discuss legal decision procedures without talking about the law, laws, legal rules, and the like. In view of the protracted debates, I want to try to make clear what I mean when I talk about law or laws. In general, when the term "a legal rule" or "a law" is used, it refers to propositions that are often of the form: "A will is not valid if it does not bear the signature of two witnesses," "A mortgagor cannot repay the mortgage debt prior to the day of maturity of the debt without the consent of the mortgagee," or "There is a battery only if there is an intentional touching of the injured person." Propositions of this form comprise what is ordinarily called the "law of contracts," the "law of torts," the "law of creditors' rights," and the like. I think, and shall assume without arguing the point, that all or most of the legal rules of this kind could be put into the form of hypothetical imperatives in which the antecedent designated a particular kind of relationship, activity, or person, and the consequent designated the legal consequences that ought to follow from the occurrence or presence of the antecedent.[36] As imperatives of this form they could serve as the hypothetical premise of a hypothetical syllogism. They could just as easily be put into universal assertoric propositions, in which case they could serve as one of the premises of an Aristotelian syllogism.[37]

Rules of this kind, however, clearly do not exhaust the kinds of propositions which have been employed by the courts and which have been sometimes called "law" or "laws."[38] For example, there are also those propositions which I call the "decision" or "judgment" in a case. They are often of the form: "The defendant must pay the plaintiff $100 damages," "The defendant's demurrer is sustained," or "The defendant is acquitted." If a court were to put its reasoning into syllogistic form, a proposition of this form might serve as the conclusion of the concluding syllogism.

Of quite another kind are the propositions that in some sense direct the manner in which cases are to be decided. They seem to be unlike legal rules (as described above) in that they are not concerned with classes of persons or activities. Rather they are concerned with the kind of justification that it would be appropriate for a court to give for any decision. I have in mind such propositions as "A case for which there is a precedent is to be decided in accordance with that precedent" or "A case is to be decided so as to effect justice between the parties before the court." I call these propositions "rules of decision" because they specify the criteria for justifiable decisions.

Finally, there are those more general propositions which attempt to state the goal, aim, or function of the legal system itself. As Roscoe Pound—among others—has pointed out so many times, an underlying principle of this kind is often neither explicitly nor carefully stated by anyone.[39] However, when articulated such a proposition might take the form: "The legal system's function is to provide justice as between the litigants" or "The legal system's function is to maximize satisfactions."

The material content that I have given to any or all of the above propositions is unimportant. The descriptions that I have given of the different kinds of propositions are far from exact. And the classes of propositions that I have delineated are neither exhaustive nor wholly exclusive. But for my purposes the above explication is sufficiently precise to enable the following point to be made. If one begins with some rather general statement of what the function of the legal system ought to be, it is then possible to consider the degree to which various rules of decision, if consistently adopted by the judiciary, would succeed in enabling the legal system to fulfill that function. By construing these rules of decision to specify the kind of justification which can and must be given by the court for any decision it renders, it is possible to examine the consequences which would follow from the adoption of different rules of decision. One such rule of decision might require that only existing legal rules may count as the justification for deciding a case in a certain way. Another might require that an intuition of the just solution must have been experienced by the judge before his decision in a case is justified. And still a third might require that the maximization of satisfactions vis-à-vis the litigants before the courts is the only thing that can count as a justification for a decision. These and other rules of decision will be examined in the succeeding pages of this inquiry.

As I have already indicated, I propose to assume that the legal system ought to fulfill some quite general utilitarian function. I propose to consider in this context alternative rules of decision that might be adopted by the judiciary. And although I propose, for the purposes of discussion, to delineate the manner in which the univocal acceptance of each of these possible procedures of justification would or would not successfully realize that utilitarian goal or function, I am chiefly concerned with indicating as precisely as I can the different kinds of decisions that would result were any one of the possible rules of decision to be adopted.

3

Some Typical Discussions of the Doctrine of Precedent

In this chapter and the one that follows the first of three types of judicial decision procedures—one based upon precedent—is delineated and analyzed. This procedure has as its sole rule of decision the rule or doctrine of precedent. Thus, in the light of what was said in the preceding chapter, the rule of precedent here functions so as to prescribe what alone is to count as a good reason or persuasive justification for any case arising within the legal system for adjudication.

This chapter considers several standard expositions of the doctrine. As such, it performs three functions. First, by presenting a representative sample of typical discussions of precedent, it reveals the inadequacies of many of the usual expositions of the theory, and the consequent importance of a rigorous restatement. A justificatory procedure based upon precedent cannot be evaluated until the rule of *stare decisis** has been carefully and unambiguously stated. And this almost all prior discussions have failed to do.

Second, a critical analysis of these theories points up the kinds of questions that must be asked about any legal decision procedure† in general and about one based on precedent in particular.

---

* For reasons of convenience I will refer interchangeably to the *doctrine of precedent* and the *rule of stare decisis* (literally "stare decisis et non quieta movere": "to adhere to decided cases and not unsettle established things").

† In the preceding chapter the ambiguous meaning of "decision process" was discussed. It should be made clear, therefore, that throughout the remainder of this work I shall be concerned almost exclusively with *procedures of justification*.

Legal philosophers have not asked these questions very clearly, and their answers have been correspondingly less significant than has sometimes been supposed. At best they have indicated the avenues that further inquiry must follow.

Third, almost all discussions of precedent do indicate that there is something important about this rule. And this significant quality —whatever it may be—may be the reason for the difficulties encountered in elucidating the doctrine. The exposition and analysis of the several discussions of precedent is undertaken as much in the hope of isolating whatever is of significance in the doctrine as of showing the doctrine's inadequacies.

The literature of legal philosophy, in general so extensive, is almost totally lacking in any systematic treatment of the doctrine of precedent. Discussions of precedent are, for the most part, incidental. There are numerous references a page or two long to the standard problems and justifications that are associated with the doctrine; and there is a considerable number of articles, many of which are concerned with rejecting the view that courts are "strictly" bound by the doctrine of stare decisis, or, more usually, with affirming the thesis that the doctrine itself permits courts to depart from prior judicial assertions, rulings, and the like. There are two or three descriptive treatises, which seek merely to reiterate the rules that courts have enunciated concerning when they will be bound by prior decisions and when they will not, and to illustrate instances in which courts have so bound themselves. But there are no full-length works that explicitly attempt to analyze the doctrine in detail or to explore its more far-reaching implications.

An examination of almost any standard discussion of precedent reveals, however, that a host of intricate, profound, and perplexing problems are inexorably bound up with any analysis of the subject. These problems have not always been recognized as such by commentators on precedent; even less often have they been resolved. Seldom have they been stated with clarity. One such analysis, by John W. Salmond, possesses the virtues of brevity and thoroughness as well as certain of the defects just noted.[1]

At the outset, Salmond reports, one must distinguish between *declaratory* and *creative* precedents. A declaratory precedent is one that a court in the past has applied to a fact situation of the same class as the instant case. A creative precedent, on the other hand, is one which—not surprisingly—is created as a new rule and then applied in the instant case. A declaratory precedent is applied because it is a precedent; a creative precedent cannot be applied for this reason, but it becomes a declaratory precedent for all future cases of the same kind. Therefore, as far as the future is concerned, there is no difference between creative and declaratory precedents; they differ solely in their relation to the law of the past[2]—to the time when they came into being as rules of law.

This distinction between these two kinds of precedents is not without importance, for it signifies an important departure from the older theory of the nature of English law. Under that theory, the view held by Coke and Blackstone, all precedents were conceived to be necessarily declaratory. Because all decisions were considered to be mere evidence—albeit the most important and convincing evidence which a court or lawyer could have—of the pre-existing Common Law, it was essential that the courts be viewed not as creating law but merely as applying that which always was and always would be the Law.[3]

It is obvious, Salmond replies, that this declaratory theory of law must be abandoned as a correct description of the judicial process. "We must admit openly that precedents make law as well as declare it. . . . We must recognize a distinct law-creating power vested in them and openly and lawfully exercised."

Having made one distinction among precedents, Salmond now finds it necessary to make another. Precedents may also be classed as *authoritative* or *persuasive*. For the purposes of our analysis what Salmond has to say about the authoritative precedents is alone relevant. But at this juncture his discussion becomes a little confusing. For he defines an authoritative precedent as one "which judges must follow whether they approve of it or not. It is binding upon them and excludes their judicial discretion for the future." Yet almost immediately he announces that precedents must be still further dichotomized; there are two kinds of authoritative precedents. When the authority of an authoritative precedent is *absolute,*

the decision is absolutely binding and must be followed without question, howsoever unreasonable or erroneous it may be considered to be. . . . Where, on the other hand, a precedent possesses merely conditional authority, the courts possess a certain limited power of disregarding it. In all ordinary cases [a precedent possessing conditional authority] is binding, but there is one special case in which its authority may be lawfully denied. A precedent belonging to this class may be overruled or dissented from, when it is not merely wrong, but so clearly and seriously wrong, that its reversal is demanded by the interests of the sound administration of justice.

Salmond's analysis is more thorough and less vacuous than many others on the same subject because he now attempts to provide a certain content for the phrase "clearly and seriously wrong." A conditionally authoritative rule of law is "clearly and seriously wrong," says Salmond, if and only if two conditions are met: (1) "The decision must in the opinion of the court in which it is cited be a *wrong* decision." And a decision is "wrong" if and only if it is either contrary to law or contrary to reason.[4] (2) Not only must the precedent be deemed incorrect or wrong, but the rule that is to be substituted must be clearly shown to be better. Salmond quotes with hesitant approval Lord Eldon's well-known epigram, "It is better that the law should be certain than that every judge should speculate upon improvements in it."[5] We may say, Salmond summarizes,

that to justify the disregard of a conditionally authoritative precedent, it must be erroneous, either in law or in reason, and the circumstances of the case must not be such as to make applicable the maxim, *Communis error facit jus* [Common error makes law]. The defective precedent must not, by the lapse of time or otherwise, have acquired such added authority as to give it a title to permanent recognition notwithstanding the vices of its origin.

Having insisted that there are certain conditions, although stringent in nature, which, if present, justify a departure from precedent, Salmond then reports that one of the most important features of the doctrine of precedent is the fact that although courts can *create* precedents they cannot abrogate them. The power of the courts to make law is purely "suppletory." When there already is settled law on any point, the sole duty of the judge is to apply that law without question to all relevant cases. The judges have "no authority to substitute for it law of their own making. Their legislative power is strictly limited to supplying the vacancies of the legal system, to filling up with new law the gaps which exist in the old, to supplementing the imperfectly developed body of legal doctrine."

What, then, is to be said of the foregoing discussion which elaborated the conditions under which judges can properly overrule precedent? In legal theory, Salmond reports, there is no incompatibility. Strictly speaking, precedents are never overruled. For in theory it is authoritatively denied that "the supposed rule of law has ever existed. The precedent is so treated not because it has made bad law, but because it has never in reality made any law at all. It has not conformed to the requirements of legal efficacy. . . . The decision is pronounced to have been bad *ab initio.*"[6]

In what sense it is meaningful to deny—even authoritatively— that a rule used by a court to decide a case never *existed*, is a question Salmond does not discuss.

When confronted with the crucial question of the reason or reasons that justify giving an exalted status to precedents, Salmond offers a rather inconclusive, vague, and elliptical answer. Precedents should be followed, he announces, because there is a legal presumption that all judicial decisions have been correctly made. Once a matter has been brought before the courts and the proper rule of law decided upon, the courts will refuse to reopen the question and under no circumstances permit it to be relitigated.

For in all probability it [the precedent] is true in fact, and even if not, it is expedient that it should be held as true none the less . . . When therefore a question has once been judicially considered and answered, it must be answered in the same way in all subsequent cases in which the same question again arises. Only through this rule can that consistency of judicial decision be obtained, which is essential to the proper administration of justice.[7]

Salmond's analysis raises, among other questions, the issue of what precisely justifies a court in departing from a precedent. The sense or senses in which it is meaningful to speak of a precedent or decision as being "wrong" remain unclarified. And the significance of the incorrectness of the precedent—for the purpose of deciding whether or not it ought to be overruled—is left unstated.

Recent philosophical discussions of the doctrine of precedent have tended to focus attention upon comparable problems. Unfortunately, the results achieved are often far from being helpful. As descriptions of the legal system (either the English or the American) these discussions can perhaps be excused for certain ambiguities on the ground that it is the legal system itself which renders consistent analysis difficult. As prescriptions for the legal system they have revealed the inadequacies of the "discovered law" theory, and perhaps have also indicated the desirability of imposing certain quite stringent requirements as the conditions for overruling a precedent. But these analyses are seriously incomplete in that they do not answer the all-important question of what these conditions and requirements are. And it is the failure to give substantial material content to these conditions which justify the overruling of a precedent that makes it impossible to extract from the theories the program for an operational legal decision procedure. Again, this is not necessarily to suggest that the conditions can be rigorously stated. But it is to suggest that at least one ought to recognize the degree to which something of significance has or has not been said.

On the whole, many commentators would agree with the import of Salmond's analysis: "A court should not overrule a precedent merely because it now believes that the precedent is wrong. On the other hand, a court should overrule a prior decision which it is convinced is palpably erroneous." Henry Campbell Black, for example, has written:

The primary idea of a precedent is that of a rule judicially established and presumptively binding. It is not to be considered in the light of a model which may safely be followed, nor as an example which will justify subsequent judicial action in the same direction. It declares or enunciates the rule or principle of law which must (not may) be fol-

lowed in the decision of similar causes in the future, by the same court
and by those courts which are under its revisory jurisdiction, or which
can be disregarded only in exceptional cases and for the very strongest
reasons.[8]

At first glance, this statement of the rule is quite unobjectionable: Precedents must (not may) be followed unless there are
very strong reasons for not doing so. Thus Black agrees with Salmond that certain strict conditions must be met before a precedent
should be overruled. Black's discussion, however, is even less in-
formative than is Salmond's because Black makes no attempt to
provide content for the phrases "exceptional cases" and "very
strongest reasons."

Another theory quite similar at times to Salmond's can be found
in a more recent book on English law, *Law in the Making*, by
C. K. Allen. The discussion, much abbreviated, runs as follows:
A judge cannot reject a principle that has been determined by
the highest court of the jurisdiction simply because the judge
does not regard the principle as being in accordance with the
dictates of justice and convenience. But there "are certain cardinal
rules of English law which are more important than the decisions
of any tribunals, and more 'binding' upon judges than any individual cases." Therefore, a judge follows precedent if and only
if it is a correct statement of the law. However, "in almost all
cases it is, to him, a correct statement of the law because it is not
open to him to set up his opinions against a higher authority; but
where it is plainly and admittedly founded on error, his obligation
disappears."[9]

The above assertions illustrate the frustrating quality of so
many discussions of precedent. Allen's analysis is quite possibly
significant; at the same time it is just as possibly hopelessly circular
and vacuous. If the argument, considered a unit, makes any sense,
it does so only by leaving important assumptions unstated and
crucial questions unanswered. Allen's statement appears to be
reducible to an assertion of two propositions, neither of which is
objectionable in itself, but whose combination—at least without
further amplification—appears to render the argument either trivial
or internally inconsistent. The two propositions are as follows.

Proposition (1): When a rule of law has been decided upon by the highest court of the jurisdiction, a judge cannot decide not to apply that rule to a relevant fact situation simply because the judge does not consider the rule to be just or convenient. Allen makes the same point again when he asserts that it is not open to the judge to set up his opinions against a higher authority. *Proposition (2)*: When a rule of law has been decided upon by the highest court of the jurisdiction, there are certain conditions under which it would be proper for the judge not to apply the rule to a relevant fact situation.

A similar conjunction is present in Salmond's analysis. Proposition (1) is implied both by his assertion that precedents cannot be abrogated and by his definition of an authoritative precedent. Proposition (2) clearly seems to be contained in the establishment of those conditions under which a conditionally authoritative precedent need not be applied.

It is difficult to determine what direction the analysis of these two propositions ought to take. Allen's assertions, for instance, are exceedingly vague and imprecise. He states that there are certain conditions under which it would be proper for a judge not to follow precedent, but he fails to specify what those conditions are. The knowledge that the doctrine of stare decisis does impose certain conditions is not without significance. Knowledge of these conditions would be of still greater significance. It is undoubtedly an overstatement—but a justified one, nevertheless—to suggest that the conjunction of propositions (1) and (2) is reducible to the assertion that precedents ought always to be followed except when they should not. This analysis is possibly unfair to Allen. For it can be argued that his premises, although not very specific, do allow conclusions and inferences of more material significance and assertoric content to be drawn; and the two propositions need not be analyzed as a tautology.

But unfortunately, when juxtaposed the propositions also give the appearance of being potentially incompatible. They clearly would be if Allen should wish to maintain that the injustice or inconvenience of a rule was a sufficient condition for not applying the rule to the relevant fact situation. For he would then be in the incongruous position of trying to maintain both that a judge should not depart from the rule if he thinks it is not just or convenient and that the injustice or inconvenience of a rule is one of the conditions under which it is proper for the judge not to apply the rule. Surely, then, one way to avoid this would be to insist that the "certain conditions" which justify departure from the rule are not to be equated with the conclusion by the judge that the rule is not just or not convenient.

The trouble with this resolution of the problem is simply that it is difficult to conceive of a criterion which would necessarily warrant departure or deviation from the rule and which would not make relevant the justice of the rule. Moreover, as Allen himself observes—and as many other commentators have noted—one of the strongest arguments against proposition (1) is that it implies a legal system in which adherence to precedent is permitted to override the fundamental goal of the legal system, i.e., the effectuation of justice.[10]

Assuming, therefore, that Allen does not mean to argue that a test different from that of the justice of the rule ought to be employed by the judge in his determination of whether the precedent ought to be applied in the instant case, what, then, can he mean by his formulation of the doctrine? He might be holding a view similar to Salmond's: the fact that a judge or court believes a rule to be unjust is not a *sufficient* condition for overruling a precedent. While this may be a *necessary* condition, other factors must be present before such a departure can be justified.

If this is what Allen means, an important issue has been stated; it has not, however, been satisfactorily resolved. Again, these crucial sufficient conditions remain unstated. Unfortunately, it will not do to appeal at this point to Salmond's statement of the sufficient conditions. For they, too, contain serious analytic defects.

The first of Salmond's two conditions, it may be recalled, was that the relevant rule be "wrong." And being "wrong" was defined as being either "contrary to law" or "contrary to reason." It is these latter phrases which provide the difficulty.

"Contrary to law" is further defined by Salmond. A precedent would be contrary to law, he asserts, if at the time that the precedent was created there was a previous precedent that should have controlled the instant case. This is necessarily a condition of being wrong, he argues, because "when the law is already settled, the sole right and duty of the judges is to follow it."[11]

This is, however, a curious and paradoxical argument. For the inquiry was begun in order to ascertain those conditions under which a court would be justified in departing from precedent. It now appears that those conditions would be met if some prior court had departed from an earlier precedent. For if a subsequent court ascertains that this is the case, it is justified in refusing to apply the "new" or "junior" precedent *on the grounds that precedents are to be followed and not abrogated.* A precedent should not be followed, in other words, if there was an earlier precedent controlling the same point. Consequently, it appears that every departure from precedent is unjustified, since it is this departure which justifies the return to the earlier precedent.

The difficulty could, of course, be obviated by insisting that only "wrong" junior precedents should not be followed. But this would only bring about a return to the question of what constitutes a "wrong" departure.

The definition of "contrary to reason" is also unspecific. A decision would be contrary to reason, Salmond apparently believes, when the court that *created* the precedent did not arrive at a reasonable rule. When courts are forced to create a new rule, owing to the absence of a precedent, it is "their duty to follow reason, and so far as they fail to do so, their decisions are wrong, and the principles involved in them are of defective authority."[12]

Who would quarrel with this position? Certainly courts should be reasonable in their formulation of rules. But once again to assert without further explication that a rule is "contrary to reason" when it is not reasonable is to say very little. This does not mean that every argument which invokes a criterion of reasonableness is therefore vacuous. There may indeed be a certain time at which certain premises or assumptions must be accepted or rejected solely on the grounds of their inherent or self-evident reasonableness. But this admission can still call into question the claim that an appeal of this kind is wholly sufficient in the judicial evaluation of particular precedents—or of ordinary legal rules.

There is one other possibility which must be considered. As we have noted, Salmond and Allen—and in fact many others who talk about precedent—may be seeking to point out that there are considerations other than the "reasonableness" of a rule that must be taken into account before a precedent is to be overruled. And there is some indication in what they say that these other considerations relate to the consequences of introducing the new precedent into the legal system. They may be suggesting, in the words of former Chief Justice Stone, that a precedent ought to be overruled only if "the evil of a decisional error exceeds the evil of an innovation."[13] Now as vague as this statement is, it does indicate a significant line of argument; it indicates considerations of a kind which might all too easily be neglected.*

The foregoing discussion of these typical explications of the doctrine of precedent has, it is hoped, accomplished several things. In the first place, the relative imprecision of such analyses as these has been delineated. In the second place, certain points of departure and of inquiry have been listed and tentatively examined. And in the third place, what could be called the *paradox* of the doctrine of precedent has been adverted to. This paradox results from a desire to bring together in one legal system two seemingly incompatible ideas: the one, that rules of law once established ought not to be altered; the other, that the judiciary should not be inexorably "engaged in forging fetters for their own feet."[14] The full impact of the paradox, though present in most discussions of the doctrine of stare decisis, remains partially concealed only because the analysis remains general and the terminology vague. But this issue should not be prejudged. One function of later portions of this inquiry will be to speak more directly to these two

---

* Chapter 7 of this work is concerned with a rather extensive examination of what might be involved in making this kind of comparative judgment. Here we should note only that such considerations may be present.

goals and the ways in which a reconciliation may be effected. Before doing so, however, it is necessary to examine a different approach to the doctrine of precedent.

The doctrine of precedent is of course not always discussed in a paradoxical manner. Many legal philosophers, Americans in particular, are very quick to draw a sharp distinction between the meaning of the doctrine in English law and the meaning it assumes in the context of the American legal system. It is interesting, too, to note that it is the American and not the English writers who insist that the English courts are never justified in refusing to apply a precedent to a relevant fact situation.[15]

To the extent to which the doctrine of stare decisis has been given the careful attention of American scholars, it has been almost unanimously suggested that there are not one but two doctrines. Max Radin, for example, suggests that there is a *strict* rule of precedent which is quite different from the American or *liberal* rule.[16] According to the strict rule of precedent, a court is bound by its own previous decisions and by the previous decisions of all higher courts. There is no provision made in this theory for the departure from or alteration of a rule that has been previously asserted and followed. The only valid justification for refusing to apply the rule is that the fact situation of the present case is not controlled by the rule, i.e., is not subsumable under the class delineated by the antecedent of the rule.

The American, or liberal, theory of precedent is quite different. "As applied in the United States, the rule of *stare decisis* is a matter of technique. In whatever way courts reach their conclusion, they are expected to place the situation they are judging within the generalized class of some existing decision."[17] The liberal rule, many authors have asserted, is one which therefore allows for flexibility and growth; under its dictates precedents need not always be followed. The doctrine of stare decisis itself, so the argument runs, allows for both definite expectation and innovations. One commentator, Judge von Moschzisker, has sought to describe the American theory in the following fashion. If a judge finds a decision which is a precedent for the case before him and

which would also fail to do justice between the parties, "his first
duty is to examine and see whether, on their facts, the earlier cases
are like the one in hand; and should it be impossible to draw a real
distinction, his next duty is, not blindly to accept the prior rulings,
but, before adopting them as controlling precedents, to satisfy himself as to their binding character and correctness in law." And if
the judge should conclude that the prior cases were wrongly decided—that the precedents are incorrect—then the cases should be
openly overruled. For if the rule of stare decisis demanded that
precedents be followed regardless of the amount of good or harm
produced in society by so doing, then this rule might be open to
the objection that certainty is being procured at too great a price.
The American rule, at least, allows the judge far greater flexibility
and thereby avoids this potential evil.[18]

In a similar manner, another twentieth-century analyst of the
American legal system has written as follows:

Case law is not wholly bound by the rules of past generations. It is a
"myth of the law" that *stare decisis* is impregnable or is anything more
than a salutary maxim to promote justice. Although "certainty is the
very essence of the law," the law may be changed by the courts by re-
versing or modifying a rule when the rule has been demonstrated to be
erroneous either through failure of adequate presentation of proper
consideration, or consideration out of due time of the earlier case, or
when "through changed conditions it has become obviously harmful
or detrimental to society."[19]

At least three considerations tend to keep statements such as
these from serving as wholly adequate formulations of the doctrine
—at least for the purposes of investigating the possible justifications
for its presence within a legal system. They are:

(1) In many instances, the so-called liberal rule is not markedly different from Allen's or Salmond's conception of the English
rule. And to the degree to which the liberal and the strict rules
are analogous, most, if not all, of the problems previously delineated recur. To say that a judge is required to adopt a prior decision as controlling only when he has satisfied himself on its "legal
correctness" is to leave the problem without even having stated it

very clearly. The notion of "legal" correctness can only be an ambiguous concept. It suggests rather strongly that the positive law is the criterion by which to evaluate positive laws, a view that the Positivists, one would have thought, had long ago shown quite convincingly to be at best unclear and at worst self-contradictory. Moreover, even if something else is meant, the truly interesting question of what shall constitute legal correctness is left unanswered.

(2) More important, perhaps, is the point that if judges are in fact bound by prior decisions if and only if these prior decisions are "correct," then it at once becomes relevant to ask in what way does it make any sense to speak of following precedent? For, if the doctrine of precedent has any significant meaning, it would seem necessarily to imply that rules are to be followed *because they are rules* and not because they are "correct" rules. For example, a recent discussion of the doctrine of stare decisis asserts that "the right to deviate from precedents is as firmly established in the United States as the doctrine of stare decisis itself, and text writers and dissenting judges who have criticized deviation from precedent in particular instances have never questioned the power of the courts to do so in appropriate cases."[20]

While there is perhaps much truth in this statement, it is also difficult to understand what the doctrine of precedent can be. If precedents can be deviated from, then the doctrine of precedent cannot be the doctrine which prescribes that precedents ought always to be followed. For if it is, then it does not make sense to say that the doctrine is firmly established in the United States, since precedents are admittedly overruled. If the doctrine of precedent is that precedents should only be departed from under certain circumstances, then the right to deviate from precedents is part of the doctrine of precedent and not a separate doctrine that is also firmly established.

(3) Perhaps one reason, not heretofore mentioned, why most discussions of the doctrine of stare decisis are so inconclusive and unsatisfactory is this: If the so-called liberal theory of stare decisis insists that a rule be applied to a particular case if and only if the

rule is the "correct" rule, then an analysis of that theory would seem to involve nothing less than a rigorous analysis of the entire process of legal reasoning and adjudication. While this is surely a necessary and desirable undertaking, it implies that there is no distinctive meaning that can be attached to the doctrine of stare decisis. It suggests that to analyze stare decisis is to investigate and describe the entire decision procedure, and it obviates the need for a separate evaluation—indeed, it precludes the separate existence— of the doctrine of precedent. And although it may prove to be true that the doctrine of stare decisis cannot be adequately discussed except within the framework of the entire decision process, it is quite a different thing to maintain that the doctrine of precedent is identical with this process. By disallowing the isolation (even for the purposes of analysis) of a distinct doctrine of precedent, intelligent criticism is necessarily rendered more difficult, more general, and less useful.

THE DOCTRINE OF PRECEDENT RESTATED

The analysis presented above indicates that the doctrine of precedent can be interpreted to be any one of three distinct rules for the decision of particular cases. These three possible rules of decision can be formulated as follows:

(1) "The rule of stare decisis requires only that the judge in some fashion relate his decision in the instant case to decisions that were made in the past." Under this interpretation, the rule is one of judicial *exposition* rather than justification. It prescribes the technique by which judicial opinions are to be written rather than the procedure by which decisions should be justified.*

(2) "The rule of stare decisis requires that the judge decide cases in the same way in which similar cases were decided in the past unless a sufficient reason exists for not applying the rule of the earlier cases." Here, a logic of justification is clearly intended.

---

* This formulation of the rule of stare decisis implies that there is some other procedure by which cases are to be justified. This formulation of the rule, therefore, is one which could be contained quite consistently within the *model of equity* described briefly in Chapter 1 and analyzed more fully in Chapter 5 below.

But, as was observed above, the explication of the phrase "sufficient reason" is a precondition of any critical evaluation of the proffered justificatory procedure.*

(3) "The rule of stare decisis requires that cases which are similar to earlier cases be decided in the same way in which those earlier cases were adjudicated." Under this interpretation of the rule it is a necessary and sufficient condition for the justification of any decision of a specified class—namely, those cases whose facts are essentially similar to those of an earlier case—that the decision be consistent with the rule controlling that class of cases.

The substantive merits, if there are any, of this third formulation will be discussed extensively in the following chapter. Certain formal advantages deserve mention here. The most significant advantage of the third statement of the doctrine of precedent is that it is neither vague nor ambiguous. This definition precludes the probability that the rule of stare decisis will be confused with

deference to the authority of the wise and just who have preceded us . . . If a court follows a previous decision, because a revered master has uttered it, because it is the right decision, because it is logical, because it is just, because it accords with the weight of authority, because it has been generally accepted and acted upon, because it secures a beneficial result to the community, that is not an application of *stare decisis*. To make the act such an application, the previous decision must be followed because it is a previous decision and for no other reason.[21]

Analytic restriction to this formulation of the doctrine of precedent provides a rule that enables its possible merits and disadvantages to be evaluated without *directly* discussing the entire decision procedure. *Indirectly*, no doubt, consideration of the legal decision process as such cannot be avoided. For it is evident that serious objections to this rule come to mind once this formulation is equated with the totality of the decision process. But if the doctrine of precedent is considered to be a rule of decision that unambiguously directs the way in which all cases of a given

---

* This is the rule of decision that characterizes the two-level decision procedure delineated and evaluated in Chapter 7. There, such an explication of the phrase "sufficient reason" is attempted.

class are to be decided, then the crucial question becomes one of determining what place, if any, such a rule of decision should enjoy within any legal system.

This third formulation of the doctrine of precedent provides a rule whose scope is sufficiently precise so that independent evaluation of its desirability is possible. It is, therefore, this statement of the rule of stare decisis which, despite its somewhat obvious artificiality, will be employed in the analysis of the first of the three procedures of legal justification now to be examined.

4

Precedent

The precedential procedure here considered is one that has only one rule of decision, the rule which prescribes that a particular decision can be justified if and only if it is deducible from an extant rule of law—a precedent. In such a procedure, rules of law are therefore all-important, since they alone constitute the valid justification for any decision. It is probably this form of the doctrine of precedent that many legal philosophers have sought to attack when they have heaped abuse upon "deductivism" or "mechanical jurisprudence." As we have seen, "deductivism" of this kind has been criticized on the ground that it cannot successfully permit the legal system to take into account the ever-present problems of a constantly changing society. Ostensibly, the consistent operation of a precedential decision procedure is so patently incompatible with all conceptions of progress, enlightenment, and self-correction that one may indeed wonder whether it even merits careful consideration.

Yet we have just seen that many consider precedent to constitute the essence of the case-law system, to exemplify all that is truly magnificent in the notion of "the rule of law." Although the thought of following rules blindly and inexorably may appear to some an absurdity from the outset, the conception of a legal system in which rules are not followed has been characterized by others as an even greater monstrosity. And, of course, it should be added that recourse to precedent has been invoked on innumerable occasions by the Anglo-American courts as the only possible justification for a particular decision.

Admittedly, the procedure of justification analyzed throughout much of this chapter is not a necessarily accurate image of the procedure that has been employed by the courts, or the rule of decision that has been approved. It does not take into account the unspecified "exceptional cases" or the unelucidated "strongest reasons" to which some writers on the subject advert. Nevertheless, the procedure here studied does preserve many of the central features of the doctrine as utilized in practice and delineated in theory. If there are deficiencies latent in a justificatory procedure of this kind, or if there are virtues inherent in it, both will probably be revealed more clearly in the course of an examination. It would be odd, to say the least, were a wholly convincing justification for a decision procedure of this order to emerge from the discussion. But it would not be unexpected should an increased awareness of relevant and persuasive considerations result.

A plethora of arguments for the doctrine of precedent have found their way into the corpus of legal philosophy. Some are serious and persuasive attempts to justify the procedure; others are thoughtful, but unconvincing. And still others are little more than paeans to the reverential implications of the doctrine. A thorough analysis requires that at least two general questions be asked. One question would inquire into the relationship between the fact of adherence to the rule of decision and the production of the result claimed. That is to say, most justifications of the doctrine of precedent rest upon the claim that its consistent application will lead to a particular end. The first question, therefore, consists of an examination of the empirical claim that the doctrine is a fruitful means by which to achieve the given goal. The second question assumes the causal efficacy of the doctrine, but calls into question the desirability of the result attainable. Being normative in character, this line of inquiry weighs the relationship between the end realized and some other goal—usually that of the function of the legal system.

Before initiating the investigation of the four major justifications of this model of judicial reasoning, it will be fruitful to pre-

sent an actual judicial decision in which a precedential type of
decision procedure was employed, and which may serve to make
more concrete and vivid certain of the implications of the model.

In the early part of the nineteenth century, Dr. Samuel John
Beamish was the owner of certain estates in County Cork, Ireland.
He had two sons, the Reverend Samuel Swayne Beamish, who was
the older, and Benjamin S. Beamish. In 1831 the Reverend Samuel
S. Beamish fell in love with a young woman—Isabella Frazer. For
reasons now unknown the Reverend could not obtain his father's
consent to the marriage. Consequently, the young lovers followed
a familiar path (a path often trod when disinheritance was a more
serious and more frequent consequence of parental disapproval
than it is today) and were secretly married. The marriage was so
secret in fact that they were (so they thought) the only two persons present, the Reverend taking advantage of his office to perform as well as participate in the marriage ceremony. Years
later, Dr. Samuel John Beamish and the Reverend Samuel S. Beamish having died, Henry Albert Beamish, the eldest son of that
clandestine marriage, brought suit in order that he—as the eldest
son of the eldest son—might inherit the estates of his grandfather.
His claim to the estate was contested by his uncle, Benjamin S.
Beamish. His uncle's case was very simple. He argued that the
original marriage between the Reverend and Isabella was invalid
because the parties were not married by a nonparticipating clergy-
man. The marriage being invalid under the common law of England, Henry Albert was an illegitimate child and as such could
claim no part of the estate as an inheritance.

To the layman the facts of this case may seem somewhat in-
credible. To the lawyer, they may only attest to the unnerving
extent to which clients succeed in enmeshing themselves in the unusual and the unexpected. Yet both layman and lawyer would
perhaps share a feeling of surprise, if not astonishment, to discover
that the case was not new, that in fact there was already a precedent. Less than twenty years earlier, the same court, the House of
Lords, had passed upon what it regarded as the identical question.
It was believed that in the case of *The Queen v. Millis*,[1] the House
of Lords had solemnly declared such a marriage to be invalid.

The following is an excerpt from the opinion of the Lord Chancellor (Lord Campbell) in the case of *Beamish v. Beamish*:[2]

My Lords, had the present case been brought here by writ of error previously to the decision of this House in the year 1844, in the case of *The Queen v. Millis*, I should not have hesitated in advising your Lordships to affirm the judgment in favor of the validity of the marriage and the legitimacy of the Respondent. The special verdict sets out a proved contract of marriage *per verba de praesenti*, intended and believed by the parties to make them husband and wife without any further ceremony. The effect of such a contract would have depended on the common law of England respecting the constitution of marriage before Lord Hardwicke's Act, which passed in the year 1753; and according to this law, I should have said, without any regard being had to the fact of the husband being a priest episcopally ordained, this was *ipsum matrimonium*, conferring on the parties, and insuring to their children, all the civil rights flowing from a valid marriage. . . . [Lord Campbell then went on to emphasize that the opinion by Mr. Justice Willis rendered in the cited case made it unmistakably clear that *The Queen v. Millis* had misunderstood earlier practice and that, therefore, the marriage in both cases would have been valid under the Common Law of England] . . . However, it must now be considered as having been determined by this House, that there could never have been a valid marriage in England before the Reformation without the presence of a priest episcopally ordained, or afterwards, without the presence of a priest or of a deacon. . . .

My Lords, the decision in *The Queen v. Millis*, that unless a priest especially ordained, was present at the marriage ceremony, the marriage was null and void for all civil purposes, and the children of the marriage were illegitimate, seemed to me so unsatisfactory, that I deemed it my duty to resort to the extraordinary proceeding of entering a protest against it in your Lordships' Journals. . . .

If it were competent to me, I would now ask your Lordships to reconsider the doctrine laid down in *The Queen v. Millis*, particularly as the judges who were then consulted, complained of being hurried into giving an opinion without due time for deliberation, and the Members of this House, who heard the argument, and voted on the question, "That the judgment appealed against be reversed," were equally divided . . .

But it is my duty to say that your Lordships are bound by this decision as much as if it had been pronounced *nemine dissentiente*, and that the rule of law which your Lordships lay down as the ground of your judgment, sitting judicially, as the last and Supreme Court of Appeal for this empire, must be taken for law till altered by an Act of

Parliament, agreed to by the Commons and the Crown, as well as by
your Lordships. The law laid down as your *ratio decidendi*, being
clearly binding on all inferior tribunals, and on all the rest of the Queen's
subjects, if it were not considered as equally binding upon your Lordships, this House would be arrogating to itself the right of altering the
law, and legislating by its own separate authority.[3]

After hearing a few short concurring opinions, the House of
Lords accepted Lord Campbell's argument and awarded the estate
to Benjamin Beamish.

Lord Campbell's argument concedes a number of points that
appear to render a justification of precedent difficult. Consider
for a moment the following four elements, all of which on a com-
mon-sense level argue against an adherence to precedence, and
all of which are present in the instant case:

(1) The opinion clearly implies that were the court to face this
issue for the first time it would adopt the rule contrary to that applied in *Queen v. Millis.*

(2) The rule in *Queen v. Millis* is confessed to be based upon
a factually incorrect understanding of prior practices.

(3) The judges who formulated the original rule announced
that they had lacked the time requisite for adequate deliberation.

(4) The original rule did not even have the support of a
majority of the court.

Despite the presence of all these factors, the court considered
itself bound by the precedent of *Queen v. Millis.* The court may,
of course, simply have been wrong in following precedent. But if
it was right—and there are surely other courts who have said and
done the same thing—there must be more to precedent than is
apparent at first glance.

THE MAJOR JUSTIFICATIONS FOR THE DOCTRINE OF PRECEDENT

Certainty

The reason that undoubtedly is most often cited as constituting
a justification for the doctrine of precedent is that its consistent
application assures to the legal system a degree of certainty which
would otherwise be impossible to attain.

It has been suggested, for example, that although an adherence to precedent may produce undesirable effects, the doctrine of stare decisis is clearly essential to a state of affairs in which the law will be certain. "Law exists," it has been asserted, "to ensure the order which the forces in control of a society desire to impose. Its object is uniformity of action, so that one member of society may know how, in certain circumstances, another is likely to behave, this being the essence of security."[4] Similarly, it is insisted that adherence to precedent is the surest way to guarantee that the future will be certain. "Because of the generality of law, men can be enabled to predict the legal consequences of situations that have not yet been litigated, and hence can plan their conduct for a future which is thereby rendered less uncertain."[5]

Edgar Bodenheimer makes this point in even stronger terms: "By applying a uniform standard of adjudication to an indefinite number of equal or closely similar situations, we introduce an element of stability and coherence into the social order which guarantees internal peace and lays the groundwork for a fair and impartial administration of justice."[6]

And again, in one of the few really thorough treatments of the doctrine of precedent,[7] the following summarization is presented: "The final, and, from the English standpoint, the most important reason for following precedent is that it gives us certainty in the law. As Lord Eldon has said: 'It is better that the law should be certain than that every judge should speculate upon improvements in it' (*Sheddon v. Goodrich*, 8 Ves. 497)."[8]

At the outset it should be observed that predictability, rather than certainty, is the characteristic alluded to by these writers; the antecedent possibility of *predicting* judicial decisions is the virtue most often attributed to a precedential decision process. What, then, is the relationship between stare decisis and the attribute of predictability?

One of the first arguments for a decision procedure that guarantees the predictability of judicial decision is the desirability of a more generalized ability to anticipate the future. Men ought to be able to predict the consequences of their actions since it is by this means that they are able to exercise a greater degree of control over their environment and to alter and shape the course of future events. Implicit in what is meant by a reasoned plan of action is the presence of a prior awareness and an evaluation of the possible consequences of alternative courses of conduct.

If it be granted that in general the ability to predict the consequences of conduct before action is taken is desirable, then it follows that those devices and procedures which enable men to predict the *legal* consequences of their actions are similarly desirable. For there are many occasions in which legal consequences are among the considerations that are most relevant to the attainment of a given end.

The importance to man of the ability to predict the consequences of his acts has also been given a psychological justification. Human beings, it is argued, have a strong craving for security. One of the most fundamental of all human needs is to feel in control of one's environment. This need can be best satisfied, this sense of security most fully attained, this mastery over surroundings most successfully achieved, in an environment in which change—if it occurs at all—is regular and therefore can be anticipated.

In part, the awareness of this need for security accounts for the presence of the doctrine of precedent within a legal system, provided it is in fact true that the doctrine of precedent is a means by which order, regularity, and stability can become the essential attributes of a legal system.[9] As stated, however, the psychological argument does not wholly justify predictability or certainty as an end. The psychological desire for stability does not in itself provide a basis for directly inferring the desirability of that end. A knowledge of man's psychological need for stability only permits the inference that the search for security may *in fact* have caused the insertion of the doctrine of precedent into many legal systems, and may be the reason for its continued existence there.

The thesis can, however, be made more appealing (as a justification) if the emphasis is placed upon the pervasiveness and centrality of this quest for certainty. That is, it is one thing to say that the desire for security accounts for the existence of the doctrine of precedent; it is rather different to assert that man must strive for order. The fact that men *must* seek to create systems in which predictability and order are prevalent may not imply that such a state of affairs is therefore desirable. Nevertheless, there is also something a bit vicious about a normative judgment which insists upon the undesirability of that which *must necessarily be*. To equate the good with the actual is to render ethical criticism meaningless or trivial. But to oppose the good to the possible is to pronounce virtue a hopeless illusion. With this in mind, the assertion of the basic need for certainty acquires more relevance as a justification.[10]

There are few, perhaps, who would disagree with what has been said. There are few who would urge that predictability is inherently undesirable. But there are many who would insist that the value of a predictable legal system is still open to serious doubt. In particular, they might very forcefully argue that a legal system whose decisions are predictable is not thereby rendered desirable, that even if certainty is a necessary condition for approval, it is not a sufficient condition. To observe that predictability is possible within a given legal system does not, therefore, preclude further examination of the desirability of the system.

For to require certainty of a legal system or of any other institution is to impose an essentially *formal* structure upon its inevitable composition. To be content with certainty as the major attribute is to demand only that results be predictable prior to their occurrence. It is to leave open the question of the nature of these results which are to be repeated in an orderly, ascertainable pattern. Like so many other purely formal requirements, it can all too easily be confused with those that are substantive.

The point is hardly original. But its familiarity should not be permitted to breed carelessness or contempt. Certainty of result may be a desirable attribute of any legal system; its presence does not assure the attribute of desirability to any legal system. For this reason, therefore, this discussion of certainty may be read as an implicit admonition as well as an explicit commendation. The ideal legal system is not proved to be ideal simply by virtue of the antecedent predictability of its decisions.

As was noted earlier, the above arguments, if they are to justify the doctrine of precedent, eventually depend upon the truth of the claim that a legal system in which precedent was the only rule of decision would in fact provide certainty. It is this claim which must now be investigated briefly.

On the face of it, the doctrine of precedent appears to be the obvious method by which certainty can be achieved. What better way could there be to ensure a regularity—and hence the predictability—of consequences than to insist that once a rule of law has been decided upon, it is to be applied without exception to all of those fact situations included within the class of cases covered by the rule? If the doctrine of precedent is strictly adhered to (and it would be in a system in which it was the only rule of decision), the knowledge of future consequences would, it seems, be possible once knowledge of the relevant rule was acquired.

Nevertheless, the truth of the empirical proposition that stare decisis, if employed as the sole rule of decision, would produce certainty has been disputed. Wigmore's analysis is typical of those which reject the causative power of the rule.

Is the judge to be bound by his precedent? This part of the question ought not to trouble us overmuch. *Stare decisis,* as an absolute dogma, has seemed to me an unreal fetish. The French Civil Code expressly repudiates it; and, though French and other Continental judges do follow precedents to some extent, they do so presumably only to the extent that justice requires it for safety's sake. *Stare decisis* is said to be indispensable for securing certainty in the application of the law. But the sufficient answer is that it *has* not in fact secured it. Our judicial law is as uncertain as any law could well be. We possess all the detriment of uncertainty, which *stare decisis* was supposed to avoid, and also all the detriment of ancient law-lumber, which *stare decisis* concededly involves—the government of the living by the dead, as Herbert Spencer has called it.[11]

There is one very easy answer to Wigmore's thesis. It is simply that stare decisis has probably never been given a test, that a legal system has never existed in which stare decisis was the only rule of decision and in which this rule was conscientiously adhered to in the decision of every case. This is true even in England. For, as Lord Campbell made plain in *Beamish v. Beamish,* a precedent of the House of Lords *can* be "overruled" by Parliament.

There is an additional argument that purports to refute the claim that adherence to stare decisis would permit predictability.

It rests upon the claim that the doctrine of precedent itself injects an element of uncertainty into any legal system in which it is the only rule of decision. For while the rule of stare decisis might permit prediction of the results of those cases for which there are precedents, it provides no indication of how cases for which there are no precedents ought to be decided. The doctrine of precedent inevitably appears to dichotomize the realm of legal consequences: in the one portion certainty reigns; in the other, uncertainty. Into which of these two areas any fact situation will fall depends solely upon the fortuity of the kind and reach of prior litigation.

There are three replies to this argument that might be offered, only one of which seems at all meritorious:

(1) It could be maintained that the above argument is specious because the precedential rule of decision does stipulate what shall count as a justification for all possible decisions; namely, it prescribes that all cases for which there are no precedents ought to be dismissed on the grounds that they fail to state a legally cognizable cause of action. Thus, the knowledge that the judiciary will refuse to give legal recognition to certain activities provides just as much legal certainty as does the awareness of the affirmative legal consequences deriving from precedential fact situations.

But this reply is difficult to consider seriously. If taken literally, it suggests that no cases ought to be adjudicated by the judiciary because *ab initio* there are no precedents. If taken to urge only that at a given time no new precedents ought to be admitted, it leaves open the question of how that particular time is to be determined. The argument was mentioned only because some courts seem, quite fallaciously it is submitted, to have refused to recognize certain claims solely on the grounds that there is no precedent for doing so. Such an argument, by itself, is self-defeating.

(2) Another reply, and one more difficult to take issue with because it is more difficult to state intelligibly, would insist that there is a sense in which precedents have always existed for every possible fact situation. Precedents are not made, but discovered; rules are never created, only applied. Since this is so, cases of "first impression" are only seemingly such. The rule for any case is "there," to be read off by the judge just like every other legal rule. The most that can be said for postulating a pre-existing realm

of *positive law* is that it does nothing to help solve the problem of antecedent knowledge of legal consequences. As an empirical proposition about things which "look like" positive legal rules but which have always existed, it is incapable of verification. And, even granting it might be possible to discover these pre-existing precedents, there are few if any persons who have been convincingly successful. Among those who do make the claim of discovery there is remarkable disagreement as to content. Whether one attempts to peer into the recesses of the Volksgeist, to look up at some "brooding omnipresence in the sky," or to turn inward toward the Moral Law, the history of mankind attests to an almost universal failure of vision.

(3) Finally, it might be argued that any precedential decision procedure requires at least one more rule of decision; namely, a rule which prescribes the way in which novel cases are to be adjudicated. Thus there would be one rule which would stipulate the proper justification for cases for which there is a precedent and another rule which would specify how novel cases are to be justified. It is difficult to see how such an addition could be undesirable.

This suggestion, however, raises once again the question of making a defensible distinction between precedential and novel cases. Of course the distinction is not clear-cut. There will doubtless be some cases which are not obviously one or the other. But there is no reason not to suppose that there will be many others which clearly fall into one of the two categories. And furthermore, as is suggested in Chapter 7, it may be true that the distinction is not significant because the same kind of procedure ought to be used to justify decisions in both types of cases.

Reliance*

The second major justification for the doctrine of precedent, although it does not speak directly to the question of the substance of legal rules, appears to present a highly persuasive argument for disregarding the material constituents of any given legal rule. For

---

* How this argument differs from the one predicated upon *certainty* will be made evident in the course of the discussion.

if the failure to provide certainty might make the legal system a
less useful social institution, the failure to give effect to those activities and commitments which were undertaken *in justified reliance* upon the pronouncements of that system could serve, arguably, only to make the legal system ill-conceived, irresponsible,
and vicious. The argument from *reliance* appears forceful indeed,
and has for this very reason invariably been appealed to as a
sufficient justification for the doctrine of precedent. Quite often
the argument assumes the following form:

"On the basis of a knowledge of judicial decisions that have
already been made and of judicial rules that have already been
enunciated, people enter into all kinds of relationships that may
at some time in the future be the subject of judicial litigation and
decision. In effect, this belief that the courts will follow precedent
has induced great numbers of people to commit themselves to far-
reaching, far from trivial, and often irrevocable courses of action.
Therefore, it would be of the very essence of injustice were the
judiciary to refuse to give anything but the same effect to these
transactions when and if they may be presented for adjudication."

Comparable sentiments are frequently to be found in the literature of judicial opinions and theory. "There is no question," a judge
dissenting from an opinion based on a departure from a precedent
has written,

that the members of the bar of this state have relied on the holding of
that case [i.e., the one just overruled by the majority opinion] for many
years and, so relying, have approved titles to property, and that under
such holding valuable property rights have been acquired. The attorneys of this state have a right to rely on the rulings of this court and
to expect some constancy in them where valuable property rights are
affected. . . . I do not base my dissent on the logic of the rule as announced in *Tillery v. Fuller* [the overruled case], but, as stated above,
simply on the fact that this court should not overrule a holding such as
this, so long established, accepted, and relied upon, which affects the
title of individuals to real property.[12]

Similar sentiments are evident in both the opinions and the
writings of Cardozo. Rejecting the argument that the rule of
Hadley v. Baxendale ought not to be applied to telegraph companies, Cardozo said:

We are not unmindful of the force of the plaintiff's assault upon the rule in *Hadley v. Baxendale* in its application to the relation between telegraph carrier and customer. The truth seems to be that neither the clerk who receives the message over the counter nor the operator who transmits it nor any other employee gives or is expected to give any thought to the sense of what he is receiving or transmitting. This imparts to the whole doctrine as to the need for notice an air of unreality. The doctrine, however, has prevailed for years so many that it is tantamount to a rule of property. The companies have regulated their rates upon the basis of its continuance. They have omitted precautions that they might have thought it necessary to adopt if the hazard of the business was to be indefinitely increased.[13]

These arguments, and many others like them, have a compelling moral quality about them. Having induced persons to act in a certain manner, the legal system could only be blameworthy if it subsequently sought to punish or in any other way thwart the previously announced consequences of action. The situation is analogous to the moral obligation to keep a promise once made. It is still more strikingly parallel to the case in which some change of position has occurred as a result of relying upon a promise. Not only have people built up morally justifiable expectations concerning how the court will regard their transaction, but they have also *acted* in such a way that they will be hurt or even impoverished if the expected effect is not accorded their actions. If, as many have argued, it is the function of the legal system to give effect to the ordinary, workaday expectations of people, is it not even more clearly the function of the legal system to give effect to those expectations which the system itself has engendered, and which have been the bases of individual conduct?

More critical examination of this argument reveals the curious fact that its persuasiveness rests in large measure upon one assumption, an assumption directly relevant to the issue at hand.

The inquiry was commenced, it should be recalled, in the hope of discovering justifications for a legal system in which the sole rule of decision was stare decisis. Reasons were sought for a legal system in which rules already formulated were consistently followed. The argument based upon the notion of reliance, however, seems meritorious only if it is assumed that there is a *legal system which is already committed to adherence to precedent.* The proposition "Justifiable reliance ought always to be given effect" is perfectly unobjectionable in any context in which the reliance was in fact justifiable. A person's reliance upon a previously announced legal rule would be justifiable if and only if that person was justified in assuming that legal rules would be unswervingly applied. If the argument is not to be wholly and abruptly circular, the fact of reliance cannot serve, therefore, as a justification for the doctrine of precedent.

The analogy to promise-keeping may serve to make the point more clearly. It could be asserted that: "One ought always to keep one's promises because promises are the kinds of statements which people can and do justifiably rely upon." The argument could then be completed by presenting any one of a number of reasons which purported to establish the *justifiability* of that reliance. But this reliance could not be justified (without being circular) merely by a showing that people have relied on promises.

In the realm of the legal system, what is it that people have relied upon when they have acted on the basis of the courts' decisions? They have relied upon the fact that the courts will follow precedents. Is this reliance justifiable? Perhaps it is for any one of a number of reasons. It would surely be justifiable if the legal system were openly committed to the doctrine of precedent. But under no circumstances would the fact of reliance alone permit the inference that a good reason has been furnished for having a legal system which ought always to follow precedent. No "promise," *ex hypothesi*, having been given that precedents will be followed, reliance *qua reliance* cannot by itself create such a duty. Therefore, although strong reasons may exist for holding that a legal system in which precedent is already the rule ought to follow precedents in every case, these same reasons add nothing to the claim that the most desirable legal system would be one in which precedents were always followed.

Equality

Although often neglected as an explicit justification for precedent, the argument from equality gives the appearance of furnishing a persuasive ground for the doctrine. A typical summarization of the apparent relevance of equalitarian theory to the doctrine of precedent is provided by Karl Llewellyn: "The force of precedent in the law is heightened by an additional factor: that curious, almost universal sense of justice which urges that all men are properly to be treated alike in like circumstances."[14] Similarly, Edmond Cahn lists inequality of judicial treatment as the first kind of situation that arouses the sense of injustice. "Regardless of the individual dispositions, the inequalities arbitrarily created arouse the sense of injustice, because equal treatment of those similarly situated with respect to the issue before the court is a deep implicit expectation of the legal order."[15]

Closer examination reveals, however, that there are at least three different equalitarian positions which might be adopted, only one of which would necessarily imply that precedents once established should always be followed.

The first kind, an *absolute equalitarianism*, would insist that all distinctions among men are, ipso facto, objectionable. In essence, its ideal society would be one in which the instances of dissimilarity are reduced to a minimum. It would follow, therefore, that any and all rules which sought to regulate the actions of any class of persons (any class smaller than the class of all persons) would necessarily serve only to create an additional distinction. The only rules allowable would be those which directed that *all* persons were to be treated in a particular manner. Ordinary rules of law would surely be excluded from this society on the grounds that they almost always apply only to a restricted class of persons, namely, those in a particular situation.[16] It would follow that the rule of stare decisis, which required that these distinctions be preserved, would have no place within such a system.

The second kind, a *modified equalitarianism*, would not adjudge all rules to be necessarily undesirable. Rather, it would insist only that any rule which has been established and applied to some person or persons must—in the interests of equality of application— be applied to all other persons of the same class. It is of the very essence of a rule that it be applied without exception to all members of the class included within the scope of the rule.[17] To make an exception to a rule is to violate this principle of equality; to alter either the substance of the rule or the class controlled by it is just as surely a violation. Consequently, a system in which the doctrine of precedent was the only rule of decision would be most desirable precisely because it alone could best ensure this equalitarianism of application.

The third kind of equalitarianism, a *prima facie equalitarianism*, would accept the desirability of rules but would not impose the condition of absolute application. Rather, recognizing the need for classification within the class of human beings, and recognizing as well the claim of ideals other than that of sameness of treatment, this theory would require only that any proposed classification or reclassification have some reasonable justification. The prima facie equalitarian principle might be of the form: "given that there is a class of human beings, it will follow that all members of this class, namely, men, should in every respect be treated in a uniform and identical manner, unless there is sufficient reason not to do so." Here "the assumption is that equality needs no reasons, only inequality does so; that uniformity, regularity, similarity, symmetry . . . need not be specially accounted for, whereas differences, unsystematic behavior, change in conduct, need explanation and, as a rule, justification."[18]

Cahn appears to regard the same prima facie theory as compatible with the sense of justice:

Courts and legislatures establish classes of humanity, categorizing for one or another purpose the duties and rights they desire to effect, to destroy, or to qualify. Thus, before a court, those only are equal whom the law has elected to equalize. The point is that the inequalities resulting from the law must make sense. If decisions differ, some discernible distinction must be found bearing an intelligible relation to the difference in result. The sense of injustice revolts against whatever is unequal by caprice.[19]

An ideal of prima facie equality would therefore not be hostile to the doctrine of precedent as such. It would, however, be incompatible with a procedure in which the possibility of presenting a sufficient reason for the alteration of a rule of law was emphatically and absolutely precluded.

These three competing theories of equality ostensibly present a choice among the goals that different decision procedures might realize. It appears, therefore, that the desirability of these ends must now be investigated. But the theory of absolute equalitarianism seems too specious an ideal to deserve much, if any, attention. And the other two theories do little else but ask the initial question all over again, i.e., what are the possible justifications for the rule of precedent? For example, to inquire whether modified equalitarianism is desirable is to ask whether it is desirable never to depart from a rule once that rule has been applied. It is to reiterate in more general terms the query: "Is the doctrine of precedent justifiable in a system in which it is the only rule of decision?" To answer that such a procedure is meritorious because it thereby ensures that all persons of a specified class will be treated in the same fashion, is patently tautological.

Similarly, to maintain that a prima facie equalitarianism is desirable because it guarantees that precedents will be overruled only for "sufficient reason" has little meaning until it is known what can count as a sufficient reason. Again, the latter issue indicates the direction of the inquiry, not the answer to it.

For the present it can be concluded that whereas these different modes of equalitarianism may restate the relevant issue in a rather different context, they do not provide an independent justification for or against the model of legal decision procedure under investigation here.

Efficiency

"The administration of justice," so the argument from efficiency might begin, "would become too difficult and tedious, and the rights of litigants left indecisive for too long, were courts not able to justify their decisions by an appeal to precedent. If a judge is not to be bound by precedent, then not only must he elucidate, ponder, and evaluate all possible rules of law which might be formulated for every case, but he must also examine all the reasons that might be advanced for instituting any one of these rules rather than any other." In short, the task of the judge would become interminable. The number of cases that could be litigated would be severely reduced. The function of the judiciary in society would be rendered infinitely less useful. Considerations of convenience or efficiency, therefore, require that the judge be provided with a quick and easy source of justification—that, in other words, he be permitted to follow precedent.

On the basis of his own experience as Chief Justice of the New York Court of Appeals, Cardozo observed that

the labors of judges would be increased almost to the breaking point if every past decision could be reopened in every case, and one could not lay one's own course of bricks on the secure foundation of the courses laid by others who had gone before him. Perhaps the constitution of my own court has tended to accentuate this belief. We have had ten judges, of whom only seven sit at a time. It happens again and again, where the question is a close one, that a case which one week is decided one way might be decided another way the next if it were then heard for the first time. The situation would, however, be intolerable if the weekly changes in the composition of the court were accompanied by changes in its rulings. In such circumstances there is nothing to do except to stand by the errors of our brethren of the week before, whether we relish them or not.[20]

Considered as one justification for the model of precedent, the argument from efficiency is both plausible and persuasive. Given a case that is clearly a member of the class controlled by the precedent, and given a model such as the present one in which the only justification for deciding a case in a certain way is by an appeal to precedent, the adjudication of cases would be both efficient and convenient. The rule or doctrine of precedent is an effective means by which these ends may be realized.

Care must be taken that this argument is not deemed to conclude the matter of the desirability of this rule. Like certainty, efficiency is a formal characteristic. And again, the doctrine of precedent is not the only means by which the specified end—efficiency—can be achieved. Cases could be efficiently adjudicated by the toss of a coin or the cast of a die; this would surely be a convenient mode of adjudication. Whether it would be a desirable method of adjudication would depend, however, upon considerations of quite another kind, namely, the kinds of results such a procedure would produce. While a degree of efficiency is undoubtedly a prerequisite for any successful legal system, its presence is once again not a guarantee of the system's value.

The discussion of these four possible justifications for a judicial procedure which contains the rule of stare decisis as its
only rule of decision by no means exhausts the list of potential
candidates. However, although the justifications still to be elucidated are greater in number, those we have examined are the most
persuasive. Many of the justifications about to be discussed seem
patently spurious. Some of them merit discussion only because
they have been taken seriously by various authors; others, still
more anomalous, tend only to support a counter-hypothesis. Most
of them are discussed and rejected in the single extensive study
which I have come across: Arthur Goodhart's article referred to
above.[21] I have relied upon his exposition to a considerable extent
in order to keep discussion to a minimum.

The Exercise of "Practical Experience"

In essence the argument from "practical experience" rests upon
the hypothesis that judge-made law enables the legal system to
adapt itself quite readily to new situations and novel controversies
by responding to these situations in an a posteriori fashion as they
arise. What this argument has to do with the doctrine of precedent
is, unfortunately, rather obscure. As we have seen, one of the
necessary conditions for the operation of the doctrine is the formulation by judges of rules of law. It can even be assumed that judges
ought to make rules of this kind. But the desirability of this
necessary condition does not imply the desirability of that for
which it is a necessary condition. That is to say, the making of
law by judges may very well be a fruitful way in which to bring
"practical experience" to bear upon the solution of certain problems. It does not follow, however, that the application of this judge-
made law to all subsequent relevant cases is therefore desirable.
Goodhart's objection seems unassailable:

It may be granted that judge-made law is more practical, being founded
on actual cases, than is statute law, which is frequently based on *a
priori* theories. To this extent it may be said that English law is especially a practical law, but—and this is most important—this practical
nature of English law is not based on the doctrine of precedent but

exists in spite of it. Practical law is law based upon experience, but how can there be further experience when the first individual case is binding? It is more correct to say that English law, being largely judge-made law, is practical until the doctrine of precedent comes into force, and thereafter becomes essentially historical. . . . Owing to the doctrine of precedent, the first experiment must also be the last.

What seems to be little more than another form of the same argument is one which affirms the flexibility of a case-law system. Here again, however, if this is a virtue of a case-law system, it is surely not a virtue of a system in which the only rule of decision is the rule of stare decisis. For although it might be quite readily admitted that a case-law system is more flexible vis-à-vis those questions for which there is neither a relevant statute nor an already established precedent, it does not follow that there is any flexibility at all regarding the justification for decisions other than those falling into one of these two classes.

This alleged flexibility of English law is, under most circumstances, nothing more than a recognition that on many questions there is no existing precedent, and that, therefore, when a novel problem does arise the judges are free to lay down whatever principle they consider desirable. There are many such vacant spaces in English law which remain to be filled, but when a space has once been closed by a precedent, then no further development is possible.[22]

Restraint upon the Individual Judge

Under this general heading, two analogous propositions are presented in support of the view that the doctrine of precedent furnishes, or can furnish, desirable restrictions upon the way in which an individual judge decides a particular case. Although neither appears to be very plausible, both have been generally assumed to be of considerable significance.

(1) The first of these propositions introduces once again that curious notion of *legal error*. Typical is Lord Coke's statement that "no man out of his own private reason ought to be wiser than the law, which is the perfection of reason." With one reservation, Goodhart seems to accept the fact that the doctrine of precedent tends to prevent a judge from reaching a legally erroneous conclusion "owing to some idiosyncrasy." He adds, however, that

there is at least one factor which might tend to negate the effectiveness of this restraint. "The very desire to follow precedent may lead to error, for a judge may feel himself bound to reach a result of which he himself disapproves owing to his mistaken belief that he is bound by a prior case which is not really in point."[23]

This reservation is undoubtedly an accurate statement of what might happen under the doctrine of precedent, although its significance is highly suspect. Nevertheless, a far more serious objection exists even in those instances in which it was absolutely certain that the prior case was in point and that a like decision in the instant case would be the only one which could be justified by an appeal to the relevant precedent. The doctrine of precedent, it was asserted, helps to guarantee that a particular judge, or court, will be restrained by this rule of decision from reaching an "erroneous conclusion" in a particular case. Assuming without conceding that the concept of "legal error" has some definite meaning, this proposition can be substantiated if and only if the following assertion is correct, namely, that the judge or court which originally established the precedent was itself correct in its formulation of the rule. Yet that this proposition should necessarily be true is absurd. There is no reason to suppose—certainly none has ever been suggested—that the court which is first forced to decide a question of a certain kind will inevitably formulate the best rule for that kind of case. And unless the assumption can be made that the precedent, when formulated, is always correct, there is no assurance that the idiosyncrasies of the judge or the court in that case have been restrained one whit. In short, if the rule was correct, then it is almost analytically true that all subsequent decisions will be correct as long as it is insisted that all similar cases be decided in the same manner. If the initial rule is incorrect, however, it also follows that the doctrine of precedent could only ensure the incorrectness of all subsequent decisions. There being no obvious reason why the initial decision should be correct (even in most cases), there seems to be no basis for the above justification.

It is significant, moreover, that if anything a fairly strong case can be made for the contrary position. For it seems plausible to assert that the later judge is in a better position than the earlier one to determine what is the correct rule of law. In particular, if the criterion of "practical experience" is to be preferred to that of an a priori determination, the later judge would have been able to see how the rule had actually worked in experience and thus to form an evaluation of its "correctness" on this basis. To the extent to which experience is required for the formation of a "correct" legal rule, the later judge is *peculiarly* well suited to make such a determination. On this basis one might argue that rather than construct a legal system in which the peculiarities of later judges are to be restrained, a more desirable legal system would result were the decisions of *first impression* to be restrained in their application. For it is the decisions of first impression, the creative precedents, which are most apt to be formulated on the basis of insufficient knowledge.

The argument is often made, however, that the opinion of the rule-creating judge is not simply being pitted against the opinion of some later judge on this question of which rule of law is the correct one for a certain kind of case. The possible controversy is not between some judge of the seventeenth or eighteenth century and a particular contemporary judge or court. Rather the argument from *legal error* has a more secure foundation. Few precedents are established simply because one judge has laid down a rule in one case. Usually a whole series of cases all invoking the same rule and all reaching the same result is what gives the precedent a superior claim to truth. It is a gross oversimplification to suppose that the rule-creating judge is presumed to be in a better position to determine "legal truth"; instead, the argument rests on the assumption that many judges and many courts have invoked this rule because they found it free from "legal error." The probability that all these judges were correct is much larger than the probability that this particular judge, who now thinks the rule is erroneous, is correct. The collective agreement of these judges over the truth of this rule is to be preferred to the opinion of a minority of one judge or court. When the doctrine of precedent is viewed in this context, the suggestion that it serves as a valuable restraint upon the fallibilities of particular judges is far more plausible.

Unfortunately, the plausibility of this revision of the justification is more apparent than real. For we have not established

any requirement that a rule must have met with the approval of
x number of courts before it becomes a precedent. And unless
there is such a requirement, unless a rule of law becomes a precedent if and only if a specified number of judges have employed it
because they believed it to be the correct rule of law, the revised
argument comes to nought. To be sure, it will quite often happen
that a rule has been applied in a great number of cases before a
given judge has questioned the "correctness" of the rule. But
according to the precedential rule of decision, this is to be expected; indeed, *ex hypothesi,* it is required. All subsequent cases
of the same kind will have to have been decided in the same way
as that initial case simply because the doctrine of stare decisis,
as the only rule of decision, requires that all subsequent cases be
so decided. Consequently, the mere fact that the rule was applied
by a great number of courts in no way permits the inference that
any of these courts believed this rule to be the "correct" rule of
law for this kind of fact situation. *Bound as they were by precedent, this issue of "correctness" was totally irrelevant.* Thus the
argument returns to the original objection. Why is the determination of the first court that a given rule of law is the "correct" rule
of law for this kind of fact situation more apt to be correct (even
in a simple majority of cases) than a determination by a later
court that the particular rule is "incorrect"?

(2) The second proposition would argue that the doctrine of
stare decisis is not only an effective restraint upon the possibility
of a later judge's reasoning erroneously, but also (and above all)
a valuable check upon a later judge's biases or prejudices.

Similar to the prevention of error is the prevention of partiality or
prejudice; thus it is said that by requiring the judges to follow precedent
we live under a government of laws and not of men. There is un-
doubted truth in this claim . . . I believe that, on the whole, it does
make for impartiality, for, as a rule, an attempt by a judge to distinguish cases which are really indistinguishable will be easily apparent.[24]

Now this argument, like the one immediately preceding, is
valid if and only if it can be assumed that the judge who laid down
the original rule was himself free from bias or prejudice. If he was
not, then the doctrine of precedent surely runs the risk of inexorably perpetuating that bias or prejudice in every subsequent de-

cision which invokes that rule as a justification. If the judge was free from prejudice, then undoubtedly the doctrine does succeed, or tends to succeed, in preventing later judges from introducing biases into their decisions. But why it should be presumed that the initial judge will be free from bias once again remains unexplained. And so long as this presumption continues to be wholly unsubstantiated, the argument remains unimpressive. At the very most, in its present form it guarantees merely that only the biases of the rule-creating judge will be operative; the number of judges who would have an opportunity to exercise their prejudices is to this extent diminished. But until we know much more about the possible biases of precedent-making judges, the weight and value of this diminution remain dubious.

The Termination of Particular Litigation

If precedent is not consistently followed, it could be argued, there might never be a final terminus for any particular piece of litigation. For once a precedent was overruled, would it not be legitimate for all those litigants whose cases were adjudicated under the old (and now rejected) precedent to seek to have their cases reopened, on the grounds that the wrong rule of law was applied in their case? If a court overrules a precedent on the grounds that it is "bad" law, does this not thereby render all cases decided under that law equally "bad"? If it does, then the litigants who lost originally ought to be able to have the case decided in accordance with "good" law.

In theory, there is nothing inconsistent about this argument. It would surely be consistent to allow all cases to be litigated every time the relevant legal rule was altered. As a practical matter, it would also be disastrous. Moreover, I do not think that a system which permits precedents to be overruled is necessarily committed to a procedure of perpetual relitigation. It would be inappropriate here to discuss the merits or disadvantages of the doctrine of *res judicata.** It is sufficient, I think, to observe that its operation

---

* In essence, this is the rule that once there has been a final adjudication of a case on its merits by a court of competent jurisdiction, this is conclusive with respect to the rights of the parties in all later suits concerning points determined in the earlier one.

within the Anglo-American legal system does not appear to be incompatible with a precedent-overruling decision procedure.

Precedent

This chapter having begun with a case from the House of Lords, it may seem fitting to conclude it with another. Yet it is not for reasons of symmetry that the following case is introduced. Rather, the case represents—in part at least—what can be regarded as the *reductio ad absurdum* of all possible justifications for the doctrine of precedent. It also serves as a handy recapitulation of many of the arguments discussed above, and as a convenient point of departure for the subjects which are next to be discussed. It is, moreover, of historical importance, since it is often cited as the one case which clearly and finally established the fact that the British House of Lords was inexorably bound by its own prior decisions. And, as we have noticed, this decision rests on a most curious argument; namely, that the doctrine of precedent, because it is operative on the House of Lords, requires the House of Lords to be bound by the doctrine of precedent. Strange as this thesis may appear, I do not think that it is a strained reading of the first paragraph of the Lord Chancellor's opinion, which is quoted below:

I am of the opinion . . . that a decision of this House once given upon a point of law is conclusive upon this House afterwards, and that it is impossible to raise that question again as if it was *res integra* and could be reargued, and so the House be asked to reverse its own decision. That is a principle which has been, I believe, without any real decision to the contrary, established now for some centuries, and *I am therefore of [the] opinion that in this case it is not competent for us to rehear and for counsel to reargue a question which has been recently decided.*

My Lords, it is totally impossible, as it appears to me, to disregard the whole current of authority upon this subject, and to suppose that what some people call an "extraordinary case," an "unusual case," a case somewhat different from the common, in the opinion of each litigant in turn, is sufficient to justify the rehearing and rearguing before the final Court of Appeal of a question which has been already decided. Of course I do not deny that cases of individual hardship may arise, and there may be a current of opinion in the profession that such and such a judgment was erroneous; but what is that occasional interference with what is perhaps abstract justice as compared with the inconvenience—

the disastrous inconvenience—of having each question subject to being reargued and the dealings of mankind rendered doubtful by reason of different decisions, so that in truth and in fact there would be no real final Court of Appeal? My Lords, "interest rei publicae" that there should be "finis litium" at some time, and there could be no "finis litium" if it were possible to suggest in each case that it might be reargued because it is "not an ordinary case," whatever that may mean.[25]

Since the only question raised upon appeal was whether the House of Lords was bound by its own decisions, this must be the "question" to which the Lord Chancellor referred in the italicized sentence. If this reading is correct, then he was using the doctrine of precedent as a justification for the doctrine of precedent.

CONCLUSION

It is certainly evident that the foregoing discussion has not established the desirability of a decision procedure in which precedents once made always serve as the sufficient justification for deciding a case in a certain way. Yet this should surprise no one. For the procedure just studied was admittedly different from that of any legal system which ever existed. Even the House of Lords, which probably follows it most closely, can have its precedents affected by Parliament. Why then spend so much time analyzing an admittedly defective procedure? Why criticize justifications that were perhaps never intended to apply to a procedure of this kind?

Questions of this order were answered in part at the beginning of the chapter. The very features that seem most to make this an exaggeration serve also to dramatize some of the necessary attributes of any completely developed legal system. And the same characteristics which seem to render the doctrine clearly an absurdity serve thereby to delineate some of the things which precedent by itself cannot do. To the extent to which the accepted rule of stare decisis requires that precedents be followed because they are precedents, it can be seen that the rule provides no criteria by which the material content of the precedents is to be evaluated, and concomitantly, that it provides no procedure by which undesirable rules of law can be altered or rejected. The decision procedure cannot be justified conclusively by the fact of reliance,

nor by recourse to fundamental principles of equalitarianism.
Neither respect for ages past nor the doctrine of precedent itself
can constitute a good reason for accepting it. This must be openly
admitted.

It is also evident, however, that a precedential decision procedure is not as chimerical as many have supposed. Even in its
most extreme form it has certain virtues. If rational activity is to
be the characteristic of any human society, then this judicial decision procedure stands for one of the surest ways by which to
make possible intelligent conduct in respect to affairs legal. If fore-
thought is to be admired and unconsidered action deplored, then
this decision procedure establishes the conditions for antecedent
evaluation and selection. The desirability of a decision procedure
in which existing rules of law would always count as a justification
for particular decisions is implied most forcefully by considerations such as these as well as by considerations of efficiency of
judicial administration.

More important, when put in the context of one of the "weaker"
forms of a precedential decision procedure, almost all the justifications considered in this chapter can be construed in a still different light as indicating something of the inherent plausibility
of the precedential rule of decision. Although none of the justifications, either singly or in conjunction, show that precedents ought
never to be overruled, they all suggest, at least implicitly, that the
fact that a court has decided a case in a certain way does make it
plausible for one to believe or expect (without knowing anything
more) that the court ought to decide a similar case in the same
way. The point, which admittedly is made only indirectly in many
of these justifications, is simply that a precedent is, for the case in
which it was originally applied, the *reason* (or a reason) given by
the court for its decision. In effect, the mere fact that the precedent was initially a justification for a decision permits any subsequent litigant to make an argument of the following kind to the
court:

"At some time in the past a case essentially similar to mine was
before the court. At that time the justification given for deciding
that case in a certain way was that there was a rule which ought

to govern cases of this kind. Implicitly, if not explicitly, that court was saying that the applicability of this rule was a good reason for deciding cases of this kind in a particular fashion. Now, unless my case is not essentially similar to that earlier case, or the reasons given for that earlier decision are not good reasons, it would be irrational for my case to be decided differently from that earlier case."

To say this may be only to restate the claim that precedents ought not to be overruled except when they are "clearly wrong," a claim that has been strongly criticized earlier in this study. Nevertheless, there is a sense in which this can be construed to be an explanation of why a justification of any kind need be offered for departing from a precedent. This does not answer the question of what will justify a departure from precedent, but it does indicate a feature, seldom noted expressly, that all precedents possess. It is possible, without talking about the need for predictability, the fact of reliance, the prevention of legal error, and the like, to notice that when viewed as *reasons*, precedents by themselves constitute justifications that require confrontation before they may be sensibly disregarded or altered. It may be nothing more than a reiteration of what others have already said, but it is at least stating the point somewhat differently, to observe that legal rules are not merely a means by which to predict future legal consequences; they are also reasons which were offered to justify past judicial action. As such, they carry their own prima facie claim for acceptance.

To recognize all this is not, of course, to solve many of the crucial problems. If there are factors that any justifiable decision procedure ought to take into account in a way in which precedent cannot, these must be specified more precisely. If there are considerations that should override the prima facie plausibility of reasons once given, these must be explored more carefully. And one way to do so is to examine alternatives to a precedential decision procedure, a task which the following discussion will undertake.

5

Equity

THE CASE FOR AN EQUITABLE DECISION PROCEDURE

A decision procedure based upon precedent, it can be argued, is an anachronism if not an absurdity. For despite the possible benefits of certainty and efficiency that might accrue from its operation, it stands ultimately for the proposition that legal rules are to be applied to particular cases simply because they are the extant legal rules. Even the most uncritical examination of the function of a legal system reveals, however, that rules should never be applied in this manner. Courts of law obviously are created to dispense justice in the cases that come before them for adjudication. The most desirable procedure, therefore, is one that seeks to ensure that all cases and controversies will be decided justly.

Were society so organized that conflicts never arose, the argument might continue, were there never "pathological cases," a legal system might well be a superfluous societal institution. But problems do arise, conflicting interests require accommodation, and as a result of acts both intentional and unintentional, parties find themselves in situations that call for the aid of some disinterested third party before whom they can place their problems and by whose authority compromise and resolution can be effected.

In a society such as ours, the legal system is called upon to resolve a multiplicity of problems and to settle innumerable controversies. It is also its function to ensure that certain standards are given effect in the deliberative dealings of man with man. The judiciary is entrusted with a delicate but almost boundless power over the lives of those persons who have been accused of transgressions against the community; it is also given the authority to decide what shall be done in those cases in which the parties have quite inadvertently worked themselves into a position from which voluntary extrication is impossible. These situations may all involve considerations of the greatest import to the litigants; they all surely demand that the judiciary function in such a way that each case is justly decided.

For this reason it is unnecessary, so the argument continues, for there to be positive, mechanically applied rules of law within the legal system. Not only is it unnecessary, but it is also undesirable. Rules of law are superfluous because it is the justice of the result that counts. Rules of law are undesirable because of the danger that they may be mechanically applied without regard for the justice in the case. The problems with which a judiciary is forced to deal, and the matters with which it should concern itself, lend themselves far better to a direct consideration of the merits of each particular case than to the sterile, unfeeling application of extant laws. Opposed, therefore, to the theory that justice requires the application of fixed rules of law to particular cases is the notion that justice means the "natural," "individualistic," or "discretionary" adjudication of each case as it arises.

This is the position that must now be examined: the view that it is both possible and desirable for cases to be decided by an appeal to considerations of justice or equity rather than by reference to legal rules.

The concept that forms the basis of this decision procedure has enjoyed a long life under a variety of names—"equity," "discretion," "natural justice," "good conscience," "fairness," and "righteousness" are all epithets that have been applied to it. This position, moreover, is one that at first sight is quite attractive, and that has at times been widely accepted and advocated. For it seems to insist from the outset that the legal system must perform precisely those duties for which it most obviously exists.

Proponents of an equitable decision procedure, as we shall see, have been both ambiguous and unspecific in directing their approval toward a process of equitable justification. But there is one characteristic about which they appear to be in accord. In all equitable procedures of justification, the necessary and sufficient justification for any particular decision consists in the fact that the decision is the *most just for the particular case.* That the decision may be deducible from some legal rule is irrelevant; that the decision in itself is just for the case is alone significant.

Examples of what have been considered systems in which justice has been administered by means of an equitable decision process are highly diverse. Roscoe Pound, for instance, suggests the example of Oriental justice. In his discussion of this "lawless" kind of judicial administration, Pound refers to Kipling's description of the court of the Oriental sovereign.

> By the custom of the East, any man or woman having a complaint to make, or an enemy against whom to be avenged, has the right of speaking face to face with the king at the daily public audience. . . . The privilege of open speech is of course exercised at certain personal risk. The king may be pleased and raise the speaker to honour for that very bluntness of speech which three minutes later brings a too imitative petitioner to the edge of the ever-ready blade.[1]

Another example offered by Pound, and one much more familiar to the Occidental way of life, is martial law. For here, too, controversies are solved not by an appeal to laws as such, but rather by the direct intervention and application of the general's authority. "Martial law is regulated by no known or established system or code of laws, as it is over and above all of them. The commander is the legislator, judge and executioner."[2]

Somehow, both examples miss the main feature of the procedure of equitable adjudication. They are, admittedly, systems in which particular cases are not decided by an appeal to rules of law. But they are also clearly systems in which there is no emphasis upon the desirability of effecting justice between the parties. They impose no requirement that he who pronounces decisions should attempt to do justice. They guarantee only that decisions will be made. The general theory of "natural justice" may have many serious weaknesses, but it surely sets a higher ideal of adjudication than this.

There is, however, one example that embodies many of the characteristics of such a procedure, namely, the system of equitable adjudication, which has played so conspicuous and so controversial a part in the history of Anglo-American law. As a historical proposition it is doubtless incorrect to consider the equity courts as a complete, self-contained institution for the administration of justice. It is surely more accurate to regard the function performed by the equity courts as only one of the several functions that the Anglo-American judicial system has in fact fulfilled.[3] Reference to the courts of equity is useful, nevertheless, because many of the adherents of a decision procedure based upon "doing justice in the particular case" have pointed to the equity courts as exemplifying the kind of procedure that is desirable. And it is a fruitful example, too, because the equity courts have at times spoken of this procedure in an equally approving manner. Thus, although to do so is to be false to the historical meaning or function of the courts of equity, I shall refer to procedures which share this characteristic as "equitable" procedures of justification.

Descriptions of an equitable decision procedure abound in the literature of judicial opinions; typical are the two that follow.

One of the most salutary principles of chancery jurisprudence is that it, strictly speaking, has no immutable rules. It lights its own pathway; it blazes its own trail; it paves its own highway; it is an appeal to the conscience of the chancellor. It had its origin in the breast of the king, who upon complaint of one of the king's subjects who found he had no plain, adequate, and complete remedy at law, appealed to his king, who thereupon instructed an ecclesiastic, the keeper of the king's conscience, to make an investigation, and regardless of the narrow and technical rules of law, mete out equal and exact justice. The Lord Chancellor became the head of these ecclesiastical or chancery courts, and thus the jurisdiction of courts of equity rests upon the fundamental principles of right and fair dealing; its creed is justice between man and man.

A court of equity acts only when and as conscience commands, and if the conduct of the plaintiff be offensive to the dictates of natural justice . . . he will be held remediless. . . . A court of equity has been said to be the forum of conscience, and an appeal directed to it is an appeal to the moral sense of the judge. In a proper case, the court acts upon the conscience of the defendant and compels him to do that which is just and right.[4]

Commentators have furnished (although not always with approval) comparable characterizations. John Pomeroy, for example,

speaks of one possible concept of equity—he finds it undesirable—
as being that theory which asserts that judges have the power

and even the duty resting upon them—to decide every case according
to a high standard of morality and abstract right; that is, the power and
duty of the judge to do justice to the individual parties in each case.
This conception of equity was known to the Roman jurists, and was
described by the phrase, *Arbitrium boni viri*, which may be freely
translated as the decision upon the facts and circumstances of a case
which would be made by a man of intelligence and of high moral
principles . . .

Charles Phelps provides a comparable characterization:

By juridical equity is meant a systematic appeal for relief from a
cramped administration of defective laws to the disciplined conscience
of a competent magistrate, applying to the special circumstances of
defined and limited cases the principles of natural justice, controlled in
a measure as much by consideration of public policy as by established
precedent and by positive provisions of law.

In describing the ideal function of the judge, Jerome Frank gives
a clearly commendatory statement of the same position.

The judge, at his best, is an arbitrator, a "sound man" who strives to do
justice to the parties by exercising a wise discretion with reference to
the peculiar circumstances of the case. He does not merely "find" or
invent some generalized rule which he "applies" to the facts presented to
him. He does "equity" in the sense in which Aristotle—when thinking
most clearly—described it. . . . The arbitral function is the central
fact in the administration of justice.

And Julius Stone provides a more neutral account:

In the last resort what he prescribed was a dictate of his, the Chancellor's, conscience—or at least the King's conscience secreted in the
Chancellor's breast. Although much rhetoric invoking the divine law
and universal justice is to be found, equity jurisdiction was based essentially on the appeal to the particular reason or conscience of the King
and his Chancellor. Again this jurisdiction was not pursued, ostensibly
at any rate, by promulgating rules binding on all men. At first, both
in theory and practice, it was enforced by an appeal to the particular
defendant's conscience, he being if necessary detained so as to permit
his conscience to operate. . . . The main difference between the Chancellor and the natural lawyer was that the former refrained from formulating in advance the assumptions on which he proceeded.[5]

The espousal of a decision procedure which ensures that justice will be done in every case is certainly commendable. Like the commitments to goodness, truth, beauty, and motherhood, devotion to justice is self-evidently praiseworthy. But to insist that justice ought to be done is not to tell us how it can be, and unfortunately, the advocates of an equitable decision procedure have not carried the task of specification very far. They seem rather to have assumed that once the goal of doing justice in the particular case has been postulated, the way in which this goal is to be realized becomes obvious. They have not indicated the nature of the specific decision procedure according to which such justice is best attained.

It would, however, be unfair to assert that nothing in the way of substantive methodology or argumentation has been offered to clarify the form and content of an equitable decision procedure. It has been argued, for example, that there are *certain features* of legal rules and particular cases that make it inappropriate to decide cases by an appeal to legal rules. Concomitantly, many have insisted that for this reason a nonrational, nondeductive method of justification should be employed. Intuition rather than reason, it is urged, should be the means by which *justification* is effected.* It should be noted, however, that reliance upon a nonrational methodology is not characteristic of all equitable procedures, although an appeal to intuition is present in most.

This chapter deals in detail with only two of the above general claims: (1) that the intuition of justice should be the essential attribute of an equitable decision procedure; and (2) that the nature of particular cases and of legal rules makes the application of legal rules to these cases undesirable. The remaining chapters

---

* Throughout this chapter the word "intuition" is used in a special sense, one that admittedly is broader than ordinary philosophical usage. For I employ "intuition" to denote any process by which truth or correctness is *directly apprehended*. In this sense it includes both intuition in the more usual philosophic sense and also such things as *emotional apprehension*. In other words, I do not distinguish between an epistemology based upon an intuition of justice and one based upon knowledge directly acquired by the "sense of justice" or the "sense of injustice." There may be differences between the two approaches, but for my purposes they can be treated as being essentially similar.

will be concerned with other problems that a reliance upon equity introduces.

As it is usually presented, the first of these claims—that an intuitive approach ought to be employed—is difficult to discuss and evaluate, for the requirement is in itself far from unambiguous, and the proponents of this procedure have provided little in the way of elucidation. Consequently, this chapter is primarily an attempt to explicate various procedures, all of which might be considered intuitive in nature. There are, more specifically, at least two distinct decision procedures that could be called "intuitive procedures" and that must be delineated and analyzed in turn. I cannot confidently assert that either of these procedures has in fact been advocated by anyone. I can only suggest that the description of these variant processes probably includes most or all of the more specific procedures that proponents of the intuitive approach have had in mind.

The first of these intuitive procedures rests upon what I shall call the theory of *particular justice*. In its simplest and most extreme form, it is the view that there is some particular feature or set of features in every case that makes it both possible and desirable to determine directly the justice or injustice of the decision in the instant controversy. The justification of any decision results from a particular intuition that reveals the decision to be just for this particular case. The second decision procedure can be characterized as a modified version of the theory of particular justice. Its basic premise is that some cases, but not all, are to be justified by an appeal to the relevant legal rule and that some cases, but not all, are to be justified by an intuition of the justness of the decision.

The modified version has itself commonly assumed one of two forms. The first of these forms, here termed the *bifurcation theory of justice*, holds that *all* members of *some* classes of cases coming before the legal system for adjudication cannot be properly decided by appealing to the relevant legal rule. The theory holds, too, that intuition must be used for those classes of cases for which rules are inappropriate.

The second form of the modified version, here termed the

Aristotelian theory of equity, insists that *some* members of *all* classes of cases coming before the legal system for adjudication cannot be properly decided by appeal to the relevant legal rule.

A third, rather different, equitable decision procedure is delineated (but not evaluated) in this chapter. This nonintuitive procedure stipulates that a decision is justifiable if and only if it best takes into account the interests of the litigants before the court. It says nothing about intuition being the criterion for justifying a decision, and it says nothing about the kinds of cases for which this justification ought to be conclusive. It requires only that such things as the satisfactions, pleasure, needs, and aspirations of the two litigants be accorded exclusive consideration in the justification of any decision.

Besides attempting to specify more precisely the nature of these various procedures, this chapter will examine the theoretical assumptions upon which they rest, and assess the degree to which some of them would in fact succeed in realizing the goal of consistently just decisions.

THE THEORY OF PARTICULAR JUSTICE

As we have noted, the advocates of an equitable decision procedure have failed to specify the way in which such a procedure should operate. It is uncertain, therefore, whether anyone has ever urged the desirability of a decision procedure based upon the theory of particular justice. Cryptic statements, which could be interpreted as adopting such a position and as prescribing its implementation, can be located. Oliphant, for example, in a passage cited earlier observed that "courts are dominantly coerced, not by the essays of their predecessors but by a surer thing—*by an intuition of fitness of solution to problem.*"[6] Judge Joseph Hutcheson, Jr., was insistent that the crucial moment in the judicial decision process occurred at the moment when the judge was witness to that "intuitive sense of what is right or wrong for that cause."[7] And Jerome Frank has offered a similar assessment. The judge should have the utmost latitude, Frank insists, if he is to effect real justice between the parties. The judge can and should respond to the unique aspects of each case that comes before him. For it is this "power to individualize and to legislate judicially [which] is of the very essence of [his] function."[8]

At a minimum the theory of particular justice as here presented is not inconsistent with these and comparable suggestions. For the theory insists that any judicial decision has been properly justified if and only if the decision has been directly perceived to be the just decision for the particular case. An appeal to a legal rule, a moral principle, or a future consequence is both inconclusive and unresponsive. The justice-creating features of the case are just in and of themselves. Once they are known by direct intuition, inquiry about justification is at an end. Until the features of the case are so grasped by intuition, all other investigation is futile.

It should be evident that what is *not* at issue is whether intuition can or should *suggest* to the judge what decision ought to be rendered. What is *not* relevant is the question of to what degree decisions are initially "hit upon" by intuition. (Or, in other words, what is *not* at issue is the question of discovery.) Rather, the theory of particular justice, as here interpreted, insists that a procedure of justification ought to be employed in which the fact that a judge has had an intuition of some kind is a conclusive justification for making that intuition the binding decision of the case. If a judge has intuited that a particular decision is the just one for this case, then the fact that this intuition was present is what makes the decision justifiable. Whether the judge suddenly "sees" *the decision* which ought to be given or intuits *that a certain decision* ought to be rendered, it is the intuition which provides the justification for the decision.

The significant features of this theory of justification emerge most clearly from an examination of what could count as a valid justification for any particular legal decision. The following imaginary dialogue between a judge and a questioner is admittedly not the kind of justification that any court has ever given for a decision. But if the language of some of the proponents of equity is to be taken seriously, it does indicate accurately the attributes that a procedure based strictly upon intuitions of particular justice would possess. The following discourse is one between a judge who has decided a case in a certain way and a questioner who is seeking to ascertain the justification for the judge's decision.

Q: "On what grounds do you justify your decision in this case?"

J: "The justification for this decision rests upon the fact that I have intuited this result to be the best possible one for this case."

Q: "Oh, you mean that there is some general moral principle which requires that a case involving this kind of fact situation be decided in this way?"

J: "No, I mean simply that this decision is just because I have intuited it to be just for this case."

Q: "But how can I decide whether or not you have intuited correctly?"

J: "Just look at all the facts of this case. Doesn't it seem obvious to you that this is the only just result? Look again and perhaps you will have the same intuition."

Q: "But if I cannot have an intuition of any kind, or if I have a contrary one, then is there nothing else you can tell me in order to persuade me of the justifiability of your decision?"

J: "That is correct. I know that the decision is just, and so does everyone else with the same intuition."

Q: "I suppose it would be fair to say, at least, that you would decide other cases of this kind in the same way?"

J: "No. I cannot commit myself, a priori, to a conclusion of what would be just in any other case. I have to have all of the facts of each particular case before me before I can properly intuit what would be truly just for that case. I can only discover what is the just decision for any case as that case is actually presented for adjudication." .

Assuming that this caricature of any actual judicial justification is true to the essential features of the procedure of particular justice, there are several grounds upon which the desirability of such a justificatory procedure may be doubted. The first of these relates to eliminating the probability of bias or prejudice in the judicial decision process.

In Chapter 4 it was assumed that the legal system ought to be free from the biases, partialities, and like peculiarities of the judges who render decisions. It was concluded in that chapter that the precedential decision procedure was a partially ineffective means by which to realize that end. A stronger objection can be made to the efficacy of the theory of particular justice in this respect. Roscoe Pound has put the point this way:

Scientific law is a reasoned body of principles for the administration of justice, and its antithesis is a system of enforcing magisterial caprice, however honest, and however much disguised under the name of justice or equity or natural law. . . . Law is scientific in order to eliminate so far as may be the personal equation in judicial administration, to preclude corruption and to limit the dangerous possibilities of magisterial ignorance.[9]

The sentiments expressed by Pound are admirable; but they require further amplification if it is to be shown that the theory of particular justice does not succeed in eliminating this "personal equation."

For the purposes of this inquiry, the assertion that certain procedures are more conducive than others to the achievement of impartiality can be understood to be either an accurate empirical observation or a defensible normative hypothesis. Those procedures, moreover, which can best achieve that end must have at least three characteristics. First, under such procedures there should be certain independent criteria by which the one who makes a decision can evaluate the conclusion reached or the course of action decided upon. This requirement ensures, among other things, that the proponent of any plan of behavior must first persuade himself on "external" grounds of the desirability of his proposal. The second, and perhaps a more significant, requirement is that the justification for any proposal should be submitted to and should be able to withstand public examination. For the prerequisite of publicity provides what has consistently proved to be the most effective means by which the enthusiasms of the advocate and the visions of the would-be seer can be measured against the less personal and more sober and disinterested wisdom of the community. To require that the grounds of a decision be made public is to insist that an avenue of independent verification and criticism be kept open. The third requirement, which is closely related to the first two, stipulates that *all* the grounds or reasons for the decision be both revealed and evaluated. It insists that the processes of argumentation, justification, and enlightened persuasion not be prematurely cut short. It demands that the process of justification continue until the "ultimate" premise upon which any decision stands and from which it draws its claim for acceptability is fully revealed. For it is only after this point has been reached that it is legitimate—if it is ever legitimate—to conclude that grounds for intelligent discussion no longer in fact exist. To urge that these requirements be present is to insist that men be *rational*—in the best sense of the word—so that the conclusions they have reached may be as accurate as possible, and the conduct undertaken as beneficial as possible.

The central role that rational inquiry and justification should play in the law has been nicely indicated in an essay by John Dewey, entitled "Logical Method and Law."

Courts not only reach decisions; they expound them, and the exposition must state justifying reasons. . . . Exposition implies that a definitive solution is reached, that the situation is now determinate with respect to its legal implication. Its purpose is to set forth grounds for the decision reached so that it will not appear as an arbitrary dictum, and so that it will indicate a rule for dealing with similar cases in the future. It is highly probable that the need of justifying to others conclusions reached and decisions made has been the chief cause of the origin and development of logical operations in the precise sense; of abstraction, generalization, regard for consistency of implications. It is quite conceivable that if no one had ever had to account to others for his decisions, logical operations would never have developed, but men would use exclusively methods of inarticulate intuition and impression, feeling; so that only after considerable experience in accounting for their decisions to others who demanded a reason, or exculpation, and were not satisfied till they got it, did men begin to give an account to themselves of the process of reaching a conclusion in a justified way. However this may be, it is certain that in judicial decisions the only alternative to arbitrary dicta, accepted by the parties to a controversy only because of the authority or prestige of the judge, is a rational statement which formulates grounds and exposes connecting or logical links.[10]

A procedure founded upon intuitions of particular just decisions does not meet these conditions. Intuitions are essentially private affairs. They are difficult to obtain; they are even harder to repeat and thereby verify. The evidence for the correctness of the conclusion reached and advanced must consist in the testimony of the "intuitor" that he has had the proper intuition. Unless one has had a comparable intuition, the word of the "intuitor" must be taken both for the fact that he has had the vision and for the fact that he has interpreted its commands faithfully. The course of human history has revealed the desirability of imposing far more stringent requirements than this in other areas of consequence; it seems strange, therefore, to argue that an institution so vital as the legal system ought to settle for so little.

This is of course not to suggest that what is needed before a good legal system is possible is an "escape from the prison house of the body" into a realm of abstract, nonsensual existences. The requirement that decisions be justifiable on rational grounds imposes no such demand. What is insisted upon, however, is that intuitions, especially if of particular decisions, should not constitute the kind of *ground* which justifies a legal decision. Since they are perforce private in nature, dependence upon them precludes any external evaluation of the judicial command. Being in essence nonrational, they can only blur the divide between fantasy and fact, between wish and ideal. Certainly it may be true that even the rational life, in this sense of the term, has not proved as conducive to happiness and freedom from conflict as some have supposed. But it is just as certainly true that the number and magnitude of undesirable actions performed under the banner of private truth and personal revelation is infinitely greater. It is surely a commonplace to observe that so long as there are men there will be judges who think they have had infallible intuitions of particular justice. But again it is also true that reliance upon the intuitive faculty as the ideal criterion of justification can only be deemed an unwise, ill-conceived, and indefensible normative position.

A related point deserves some mention, if not discussion. It was seen in Chapter 4 that the possibility of antecedent prediction of judicial consequences was a significant and desirable attribute for a legal system to possess. This goal, too, seems singularly unattainable by the kind of intuitive theory of justification presented here. If the judge is to adjudicate cases on the basis of what is just *in the particular case,* and solely in the light of the uniqueness of that case, then three things follow: first, the task of classification becomes increasingly difficult, if not impossible; second, because the *particularity* of the situation is what is crucial, past decisions are, *ex hypothesi*, extremely unreliable guides for future judicial action; and third, to the extent to which intuitions are apt to be peculiar to a particular judge, the path of adjudication is rendered still more wavering and unpredictable.

It could be argued that the justice-making conditions of particular cases need not be different in every case. But if this is so, it is hard to see why proponents of the theory of particular justice insist that it is the *unique* factors of each case that are truly significant. It is also possible to argue that independent verification might be achievable because other people can have the same intuition of particular justice and thereby test the original conclusion's correctness. But if so, then the empirical thesis upon which this claim rests ought to be demonstrated quite convincingly before it is accepted—particularly in the light of the extensive historical evidence to the contrary.

The failure of the theory of particular justice to provide a means by which a decision can be tested on rational grounds, or sufficient legal data from which rational inferences about the future can successfully be made, constitutes one of the more serious limitations upon the possible value of such a theory of justification. Equally important is the previously postulated inherent unreliability of particular intuitions. If the theory of equity implies the acceptance of a procedure such as this (and of course it need not), there are, it is submitted, reasons more than sufficient to justify its rejection.

MODIFIED THEORIES OF PARTICULAR JUSTICE

That all decisions ought to be fully justified solely by an intuition of the justice of the decision is admittedly an extreme position. It is perhaps inaccurate even to attribute its advocacy to any particular legal philosopher. But there are two restricted or modified versions of the theory of particular justice which have been quite explicitly formulated and widely accepted. On the one hand, the *bifurcation theory of justice,* urged most consistently by Roscoe Pound, insists that there is a fundamental distinction between two

kinds of cases, namely those which relate to matters of property
and contract, and those which involve conflicts of human conduct
and enterprises. The former class of cases should, Pound insists,
be decided by appeal to rule; the latter class by appeal to intuition.
The *Aristotelian theory of equity,* on the other hand, holds that
legal rules ought to be used to decide cases of all kinds, but that
within every class of cases there are some particular cases to which
legal rules are *necessarily* inapplicable.

Both theories raise two questions: (1) Why should rules of
the form of ordinary legal rules not be used to decide all cases
coming before the courts for adjudication? and (2) How should
those cases which should not be decided by appeal to legal rules
be decided? Because neither Pound nor Aristotle has provided a
convincing argument in support of the dichotomies proposed, the
first question will be the focal point of the discussion. The theories
are studied essentially for the arguments offered in support of the
thesis that at least some cases ought to be decided by appeal to
something other than the relevant legal rule which has been or
which could be formulated. However, to the extent to which they
suggest a different way in which cases of this kind ought to be
decided, these procedures are also analyzed.

The Bifurcation Theory of Justice

The clearest and most complete statement of the bifurcation
theory is found in a lengthy article by Pound, entitled "The Theory
of Judicial Decision." Here, relying heavily upon his own interpretation of Henri Bergson's metaphysics, Pound proposes that
cases involving contract and property rights be decided by rules
and abstract conceptions. And he proposes that cases which are
concerned with human conduct ought to be dealt with intuitively.

We should not be ashamed, Pound insists, to admit that intuition should play the decisive role in the adjudication of cases involving human life.

Bergson tells us that intelligence, which frames and applies rules,
is more adapted to the inorganic, while intuition is more adapted to life.
In the same way rules of law and legal conceptions which are applied
mechanically are more adapted to property and to business transactions;

standards where application proceeds upon intuition are more adapted to human conduct and to the conduct of enterprises. Bergson tells us that what characterizes intelligence as opposed to instinct is "its power of grasping the general element in a situation and relating it to past situations." But, he points out, this power is acquired by loss of "that perfect mastery of a special situation in which instinct rules." Standards applied intuitively by court or jury or administrative officer, are devised for situations in which we are compelled to take circumstances into account; for classes of cases in which each case is to a large degree unique. For such cases we must rely on the common sense of the common man as to common things and the trained common sense of the expert as to uncommon things. Nor may this common sense be put in the form of a syllogism. To make use once more of Bergson's discussion of intelligence and instinct, the machine works by repetition; "its use is mechanical and because it works by repetition there is no individuality in its products." The method of intelligence is admirably adapted to the law of property and to commercial law, where one fee simple is like every other and no individuality of judicial product is called for as between one promissory note and another. On the other hand, in the hand-wrought product the specialized skill of the workman, depending upon familiar acquaintance with particular objects, gives us something infinitely more subtle than can be expressed in rules. In the administration of justice some situations call for the product of hands not of machines. Where the call is for individuality in the product of the legal mill—*i.e.*, where we are applying law to human conduct and to the conduct of enterprises—we resort to standards and to intuitive application.[11]

The foundation offered by Pound for the bifurcation of cases is this: One fee simple or one promissory note is like every other one of the same class. Consequently, each can be treated like every other. Any case involving human conduct is essentially different from every other one. Consequently, each must be treated intuitively on its own merits and peculiar facts.[12] The dichotomy, when based upon this rationale, is untenable. In order to demonstrate wherein lies the fallacy of Pound's argument and in order to be certain that he is not being misinterpreted, an acceptable example of each of the two kinds of cases must first be given.

Examples of the first kind of case are plentiful. I assume that Pound would accept the following as an illustration of the kind of property or contract case that should be adjudicated mechanically or conceptually. *A*, the owner of Blackacre in fee simple, has leased Blackacre to *B* for one year for a yearly rental of $5,000. At the end of the year, despite *A*'s insistent pleas, *B* fails to vacate the premises and remains in possession of Blackacre after the expiration date of the lease. *A* sues *B* for $5,000, claiming that since *B* "held over" beyond the time of the original rental period, *A* can treat *B* as a tenant for another term—in this case one year—and recover the rental for that term.

I am not so confident that I can locate a clear-cut example of the second kind of case. I think, however, that Pound would agree that the following exemplifies the type of case that manifestly called for intuitive adjudication because it had circumstances which required individualized treatment.

On July 8, 1916, Harvey Hynes, a lad of sixteen, swam with two companions from the Manhattan to the Bronx side of the Harlem river or United States Ship Canal, a navigable stream. Along the Bronx side of the river was the right of way of the defendant, the New York Central railroad, which operated its trains at that point by high tension wires, strung on poles and crossarms. Projecting from the defendant's bulkhead above the waters of the river was a plank or springboard from which the boys of the neighborhood used to dive. One end of the board had been placed under a rock on the defendant's land, and nails had been driven at its point of contact with the bulkhead. . . . For more than five years swimmers had used it as a diving board without protest or obstruction.

On this day Hynes and his companions climbed on top of the bulkhead intending to leap into the water. One of them made the plunge in safety. Hynes followed to the front of the springboard, and stood poised for his dive. At that moment a crossarm with electric wires fell from the defendant's pole. The wires struck the diver, flung him from the shattered board, and plunged him to his death below. His mother, suing as administratrix, brings this action for her damages.[13]

Assuming that Pound would accept these as typical of the two kinds of cases distinguished, he might argue by way of clarification that they should be so distinguished on the following grounds. In the case between *A* and *B* there was a perfectly valid written lease between the parties, under which *B* was only entitled to the premises for one year. By refusing to vacate by the termination date of the lease, *B* became a "hold-over" tenant. A hold-over in this case is no different from a hold-over in any other case. Consequently, *B*'s rights should be no different from any other hold-over tenant's, and *A* should, therefore, be able to recover the rental for the entire term.

The case of poor Harvey Hynes is essentially different. All sorts of imponderables are present in such a case, and because they are imponderables, they cannot be clearly specified. Although only approximations of the nature of *this* case, the fact that Harvey was a poor city boy who had nowhere else to swim, the fact that he and his friends had been swimming there for years, the fact that the defendant was a wealthy railroad, and the fact that it probably knew the boys had been swimming there, all go to make this particular case the kind that should not be decided by the mechanical application of the rules of trespasser-landowner liability.

When stated in this fashion, Pound's bifurcation has ostensive persuasiveness. The comparison of one lease with another lease, one can argue, does not reveal any significant differences between them; the respective positions of Harvey Hynes and the New York Central Railroad, when put in the particular context of Harvey's death, seem to make a special case. The persuasiveness of the dichotomy lies not in any substantial difference between two kinds of cases, however, but rather in the way in which the two cases are described. The superficiality of the supposed essential distinction can be demonstrated most dramatically by reporting the two cases at issue in a quite different fashion. Instead of merely announcing that there was a properly executed lease between two unnamed persons—two letters—*A* and *B*, the so-called "property" kind of case can be described in the following manner. The lessee, Herter by name, admits that he was to vacate the lessor's dwelling house on May 1, 1895. But on May 1, 1895, Herter's mother, who lived in the house with him, was afflicted with a disease which

confined her to her bed so that it would have endangered her life to take her from the house; that for that reason, and no other, of which the plaintiff [lessor] had full knowledge and notice, the defendants were obliged to and did occupy a small portion of the premises until May 15th; that all their property, furniture and belongings and their family were removed from the premises, and every part thereof, on May 1, 1895, except from the sick room in which their mother was confined, and that they were forbidden by the physician in charge to remove her until May 15th, when she was at once removed.[14]

In the same manner, the *Hynes* case can be presented in an impersonal fashion: *A*, a trespasser upon *B*'s land, was killed when an electric wire, necessary to the operation of *B*'s business, fell from its point of attachment and struck the trespasser. The trespasser's estate sues the landowner, *B*, for damages.

The point of these two restatements is simply this. It seems just as plausible to argue that one trespass is like any other trespass as it does to argue that one lease is like any other lease. If one looks only to the "transaction" and not to the parties to the transaction, a "mechanical" application of rule to transaction seems precisely as sensible in the one case as in the other. Conversely, if one looks to the "special circumstances" of a case, just as many special circumstances may constitute a property case as a tort case.

The conclusion is not that "special circumstances" ought never to be taken into account, nor that all cases ought to be decided "mechanically." Rather, it is simply that the differentiation of cases *on the grounds that all property cases are alike whereas all tort cases are different* cannot be intelligently sustained. There may indeed be good reasons for treating property and contract cases in one way, and cases like the *Hynes* case in a different way. Some of these reasons are discussed in the next chapters. But to assert that the realm of legal cases should be bifurcated for the reason given by Pound just does not make sense. If one should decide not to consider the special circumstances in property cases but to consider them in tort cases, then of course there will be a difference between the two kinds of cases. The fact remains, nevertheless, that special circumstances are present in any property case precisely to the same extent to which they are present in any other case that might require adjudication. A lease is no more and no less unique than a trespass. Circumstances can be taken into account just as sensibly in the one kind of case as in the other. If the two kinds of cases ought to be treated differently, it is not because there is anything *inherently* different about either class. Thus, if the bifurcation is to be allowed to stand, some other substantiation must be forthcoming.

Similarly, there may be nothing objectionable in suggesting, as Pound does, that there are some cases which ought to be decided by an appeal to different kinds of rules than the rules used to justify other decisions. It is probably of considerable significance to observe that there are some kinds of cases that can best be decided by rules which themselves contain reference to some very general standard rather than to some more narrow set of conditions. This appears to be what Pound has in mind when he says:

> Frequently application of the legal precept, as found and interpreted, is intuitive. This is conspicuous when a court of equity judges of the conduct of a fiduciary, or exercises its discretion in enforcing specific performance, or passes upon a hard bargain, or where a court sitting without a jury determines a question of negligence. However repugnant to our nineteenth century notions it may be to think of anything anywhere in the judicial administration of justice as proceeding otherwise than on rule and logic, we cannot conceal from ourselves that in at least three respects the trained intuition of the judge does play an important rôle in the judicial process. One is in the selection of grounds of decision—in finding the legal materials that may be made both to furnish a legal ground of decision and to achieve justice in the concrete case. It is an everyday experience of those who study judicial decisions that the results are usually sound, whether the reasoning from which the results purport to flow is sound or not. The trained intuition of the judge continually leads him to right results for which he is puzzled to give unimpeachable legal reasons. Another place where the judge's intuition comes into play is in development of the grounds of decision, or interpretation. This is especially marked when it becomes necessary to apply the criterion of the intrinsic merit of the possible interpretations. A third is in application of the developed grounds of decision to the facts.[15]

Like so many discussions of the role of intuition, the above quotation is more than a little perplexing. Perhaps Pound is correct in suggesting that tort cases, for instance, are and ought to be decided by an appeal to a standard of reasonableness rather than by reference to particular rules which specify with greater precision what shall and shall not be reasonable conduct. (This is a matter which is discussed in greater detail in Chapter 7.) But even if this is what Pound means, it does not follow that two different "kinds" of justification ought to be employed *because* there are two fundamentally different kinds of cases, i.e., those which are essentially similar one to another and those which are inherently unique.

Furthermore, it is hard to understand what it means to say

that the grounds of decision are and ought to be selected intuitively. If this means that the only justification which can be given for supporting a decision on a certain ground is that the judge intuited the ground to be appropriate for the decision, then the intuitive selection of grounds seems open to the same criticism made earlier of the intuitive selection of particular decisions. And in this connection it is even more difficult to comprehend how developed grounds are to be applied intuitively to facts. For if there is one place in which logic—in the narrow or formal sense—seems directly applicable, it is in the application of rules or grounds to the particular fact situations already described.

Again, if it is correct to say that there are cases in which a general standard, rather than a legal rule, ought to be appealed to, it does not follow that the appeal need be intuitive in nature. Even if there are cases in which the crucial question is one of whether conduct was reasonable or unreasonable, it is not obvious that this is the kind of question which cannot be answered "rationally." Pound's remarks are at least open to the interpretation that if a general standard is to be applied to conduct, the only thing which can be said about that conduct is that the activity was intuited to be reasonable or unreasonable. Yet it does seem that reasons of a nonintuitive kind can be given to support a view that conduct was or was not reasonable in the light of a particular standard. Indeed, it is difficult to understand what role the standard is to play in the process of justification if it is to be taken into account only intuitively.

And finally, if Pound is correct in asserting that judges have "reached the right results" even though they have given the wrong reasons, then he seems here to be suggesting that there are "right reasons" which could and should have been given. Now perhaps all he means by a right reason is an intuition of the correctness of the decision. But if he means something else, if he means that there are other criteria by which the "rightness" of a decision can be evaluated, then it would seem that it is *these* criteria, rather than intuition, which ought to be explicated. The fact that courts have often given "wrong reasons" does not by itself imply that reasons ought not be given. And if it makes sense to talk about the "rightness" or "wrongness" of judicial decisions (in some nonintuitive sense), this would seem to imply that there are reasoned justifications that courts could and should have given for their decisions. It is these reasons that the courts should have given but did not give which ought to count as the proper justification for deciding a case in a certain fashion. And whatever it is that makes these reasons "good" ought to be made the criteria of justification. Thus, although there may be some purpose in retaining Pound's bifurcation, the justification for retaining it remains unstated. And although it may be useful to observe that some cases ought to be decided by appealing to a standard rather than a rule, this does not imply that intuition ought to be the criterion of either their correct selection or their application.

The Aristotelian Theory of Equity

The acceptance of an argument like Pound's is not uncommon. Far more usual, however, is the recourse to an argument based upon the thesis that rules cannot properly be employed to decide *all* cases of any *class*. There will always be, it is insisted, *some* members of any class for which the application of the desirable legal rule is inappropriate. Legal rules simply cannot take an adequate account of all cases of any kind; some cases must be decided by a direct appeal to considerations of justice.

Such a view has been accepted quite uncritically by almost all commentators upon and philosophers of the law as well as by many courts.[16] The *locus classicus* of this position is Chapter 10, Book v, of the *Nicomachean Ethics*; in more recent sources, Aristotle's language is repeated with only a minimum of alteration. As stated by Aristotle and reiterated by subsequent philosophers, the justification for this hypothesis is, I submit, without substantial foundation. But deference to both its author and its widespread acceptance requires that the proposal be given careful consideration.

Aristotle begins by distinguishing between two kinds of justice: legal justice and some other form of justice with which equity is perhaps to be equated. This distinction is necessary because, says Aristotle, there is something about the generality of rules which makes it incorrect to identify completely justice with rules. The reason this is so

is that all law is universal but about some things it is not possible to make a universal statement which shall be correct. In those cases, then, in which it is necessary to speak universally, but not possible to do so correctly, the law takes the usual case, though it is not ignorant of the possibility of error. And it is none the less correct; for the error is not in the law nor in the legislator but in the nature of the thing, since the matter of practical affairs is of this kind from the start . . . Hence the equitable is the just, and better than one kind of justice—not better than absolute justice but better than the error that arises from the absoluteness of the statement. And this is the nature of the equitable, a correction of law where it is defective owing to its universality. In fact this is the reason why all things are not determined by law, viz. that about some things it is impossible to lay down a law, so that a decree is needed.[17]

It should be evident that this passage reveals a reliance upon some of the theories and problems with which this analysis has already dealt. But Aristotle's statement also presents several new issues; in particular, these conditions under which a relevant rule ought not to be applied to a particular fact situation must be formulated and evaluated more precisely. There appear to be two possible interpretations of what Aristotle has in mind.

On the one hand, the passage might be construed to be merely putting forth the view that there will always be some cases that will not have been envisioned ahead of time by a legislator. This might be what Aristotle means when he says: "When the law speaks universally, then, and a case arises on it which is not covered by the universal statement, then it is right, where the legislator fails us and has erred by oversimplicity, to correct the omission— to say what the legislator himself would have said had he been present, and would have put into his law if he had known."[18] The Swiss Civil Code appears to follow Aristotle's advice here. "The Law must be applied in all cases which come within the letter or the spirit of any of its provisions. Where no provision is applicable, the judge shall decide according to existing Customary Law and, in default thereof, according to the rules which he would lay down if he had himself to act as legislator."[19] If, in other words, a case arises for which there is no relevant legal rule, then the judge clearly must look to something other than the set of positive rules for the justification for his decision.

For example, there is not at present any relevant law on the subject of drivers' licenses for interspace vehicles. The legislator—and here it is immaterial whether he be the legislator *qua* legislator or the judge *qua* legislator—would quite understandably not have enacted such a law simply because there does not, at present, appear to be any need to regulate such a class of occurrences. And there doubtless is a limitless number of classes of cases which at any given time cannot be foreseen and therefore legislated about simply because the existence of any of their members has not yet been envisioned.

On the other hand, it is also apparent that this is not the real import of Aristotle's point. On the contrary, the first passage quoted above rests on quite a different supposition. It seems to depend upon the premise, also crucial to Pound's bifurcation theory and to the theory of particular justice, that there are at least some situations that are *simply not amenable to general rules of any kind.* In at least three different places Aristotle comments on this point: "about some things it is not possible to make a universal statement which shall be correct"; "the error is not in the law nor in the legislator but in the nature of the thing"; "about some things it is impossible to lay down a law."

These passages, in turn, would once again appear to support two different interpretations. (1) Aristotle might mean that there are certain classes of acts or situations about which rules ought not to be laid down at all. The characteristics of some kinds of cases do not justifiably permit of that abstraction and classification necessary for the adjudication of particular cases by means of ordinary legal rules. Aristotle might, that is, be suggesting a theory very much like Pound's: There are fundamentally two different kinds of classes of cases.

(2) There is, however, another more plausible interpretation of these same statements. The passages appear to imply that for any given general rule which prescribes how any member of a class of cases is to be treated, there will always be some particular fact situation which is indisputably a member of that class of situations,

but which nevertheless ought not to be treated in accordance with
that law. This interpretation has been accepted by modern theorists as the explanation for the so-called hardship case.

In many of the hardship cases some characteristic of the individual
claimant's situation which indicates weakness (but which is legally irrelevant in private law under the principle of "equality before the law")
arouses sympathy for him or her: The widow who bought from the
banker her deceased husband's worthless note, giving her valuable
promise; the poor city youth who found his precarious recreation on
the springboard projecting over the river from the wealthy railroad's
right-of-way; the poor manual worker who loyally crippled himself for
life in order to save his employer from injury; a veteran of a recent war,
seeking a desperately needed home for his family and himself, [who]
made a contract on Sunday for the purchase of a house.[20]

It is this second interpretation of Aristotle which calls for careful analysis.

The most troublesome feature of the theory centers about the
claim that the fault lies not in the general laws. Aristotle does not
appear to argue that the law was improperly or incorrectly formulated, that, in other words, the legislator failed to take into account
certain factors which should have been considered. Nor does he
rest his claim upon the premise that there are certain borderline
cases in which classification is extremely difficult and in which,
therefore, there is always the possibility that an unjust result will
be reached because the case was not in fact properly a member of
the class controlled by the rule. The problem, in short, is neither
one of insufficient legislative competence nor one of incorrect
judicial application. Rather, the claim appears to be that regardless of the care with which any law may be drafted, it is not possible that it can adequately take into account all relevant cases.

If the latter interpretation is correct, the theory is bewildering
simply because it is so difficult to envision a substantiating example. While one can think, for example, of hundreds of cases in
which an "unjust" result might be reached by applying a given
rule to a case, one cannot think of a single instance in which a rule
could not be formulated that would cover the instant case and all
other cases of the same kind in such a way as to produce a just
result in all cases. If Aristotle is saying merely that *for any given*

set of rules, it will probably happen that some unjust results will occur when these rules are applied in all relevant instances, then the thesis is unobjectionable. But if something more is meant, if it is insisted that the continual revision of the rules would still not alleviate the problem, then the theory is less intelligible. For it seems always theoretically possible to formulate a rule whose classification would be sufficiently restrictive to exclude all cases in which an "unjust" result might be produced. Another way to make the same point is to observe that in theory to make an exception to a rule is simply to introduce two more restrictive rules in place of the original.

Reference to one of the "hardship cases" may help to clarify the issue. The case of Webb, the devoted employee, is typical.[21] Webb was at work on one of the upper floors of the Smith Company Lumber Mill. He was clearing the floor of scrap wood. The usual and accepted way of doing this was by dropping the wood down to the floor below. As he was just about to drop a 75-pound block of pine, Webb saw that his employer, J. Greely McGowin, was standing directly on the spot that would be hit by the block if it were to fall straight down. The only way by which Webb could prevent McGowin from being seriously injured was for him, Webb, to divert the block from its course of fall; and the only way he could reasonably do this was by falling to the ground with the block. This is precisely what he did. He saved McGowin from harm but only at the cost of inflicting serious injury upon himself. He was, in fact, badly crippled for the remainder of his life.

McGowin, understandably grateful, soon entered into an agreement with Webb whereby he promised to pay Webb $15 every two weeks for the remainder of Webb's life in gratitude for Webb's courageous act. McGowin did this up until the time of his death. His estate continued the payments for another three years and then stopped them even though Webb was still alive. The problem confronting the court when Webb brought suit to compel the estate to continue payment was this: There was a rule of long standing which held that a promise is binding upon the promisor if and only if it is given in exchange for services which have yet to be performed or for a promise to perform some act in the future. In other words, the fact that Webb acted with no prior request from McGowin, coupled with McGowin's subsequent promise to pay Webb for his past injuries, amounted to a mere "past" or "moral" consideration, the kind of consideration which could not support a legal action to enforce performance of that promise.

Let it be assumed that Webb ought to be able to enforce Mc-Gowin's agreement and that an unjust result would be reached if he were not allowed to do so. Let it also be agreed that to apply the extant rule to this case would produce an unjust result. To grant these two premises is still not to grant Aristotle's point. Why, if it is unjust not to give legal effect to this agreement, is this not a *kind* of case for which a rule could be formulated that would be capable of producing a just result if applied to all cases of this class? For example, a rule such as the following might be introduced: "Whenever an employee engaged in a proper course of conduct finds that the only way he can reasonably prevent serious injury to his employer is by injuring himself, and whenever a promise is made thereafter by the person saved from injury to pay that person for his injury, this promise is enforcible." It is difficult to find anything which *in theory* requires the inference that if this rule were to be applied to all members of the specified class, some unjust results would necessarily be produced. As will become evident in a moment, there may be weaknesses inherent in rules of this specificity; but the difficulties are practical rather than theoretical. The issue here is simply that there is nothing which *in principle* prevents a situation such as the one Webb found himself in from being treated as one of a definite class of situations. And if it can be treated as a member of one or more classes, then, again, there is nothing in principle that precludes the formulation of a rule which could produce just results when applied to every member of that class.

The plausibility of a view such as Aristotle's derives in part perhaps from a confusion between two different concepts—from the failure to distinguish what I shall call a law's *universality* from its *generality*. To say that a law is or should be *universal* is simply to assert that the law applies without exception to all the members of the class included within the scope of the law. To speak of the universality of law is to refer to that feature which renders the law applicable to every member of the specified class. A strong case can be made for the analytic truth of the proposition that all laws are universal in this sense.

The generality of a law is something quite different. To speak of a law's generality is to observe the degree to which the class which is governed by the law is discriminated from all other possible classes. The generality of a law is concerned, therefore, with the particular class which is named and controlled by the law; universality, on the other hand, is concerned with the way in which the law is to be applied to the members of the class. Universality is a formal characteristic; generality is a material one.

An adherence to this distinction permits more meaningful discussion of the Aristotelian thesis and its implications. For it becomes obvious that the most important problems it raises center about the generality rather than the universality of rules. That all laws should be universal seems evident; that all laws should be of *any particular* generality is far less certain. Two competing considerations are relevant to the question of what constitutes the desirable generality of ordinary rules of law.

First, if all rules of law were absolutely general, i.e., if they dictated the same result for every member of the class consisting of all persons, the number of substantively unjust results would undoubtedly be very great. For as was observed above, it is only as the generality of the rule is "contracted" that the chance of just results in every case increases. As more conditions are placed upon membership in the class controlled by the rule, it becomes increasingly unlikely that an "exceptional" case will arise.

Second, and serving to support the contrary hypothesis that legal rules should "expand" their generality, is the consideration that as rules become too specific their utility *qua* rules diminishes. That is, although the proposed rule for the Webb type of situation may be sufficiently "narrow" so that injustices will not result, it is also so specific that it enables prediction of very few cases. The issue here is wholly analogous to one raised earlier. Rules are useful because they enable one to predict a legal result in advance. But if the rule applies only to a very limited class, if its generality is minimal, then knowledge of the rule does not permit the accurate prediction of many cases. Concomitantly, a minimal generality requires—if prediction is to be possible—a proliferation of rules. Because each rule controls only a small class, many rules are needed to take account of all cases. A mastery of the content of a great number of rules becomes a precondition of successful prediction.

Thus in a different context, Aristotle's position is not without significance. Theoretically, the thesis is untenable. Given an indefinitely large number of rules there is no reason why all cases could not be decided justly by means of an appeal to rules. But as a practical matter, rules cannot become too specific and still fulfill their most important function as rules. The number of rules cannot be multiplied indefinitely without creating a comparable impairment of function. Thus if the rules of a legal system are to be general enough to function properly as rules, there is good reason to suppose that they might not be able to take an adequate account of all cases controlled by the rules. Whether this latter consideration requires the rejection of a rule-applying logic of justification is the question with which Chapter 7 is chiefly concerned.

Before we leave the question of minimal generality one point deserves some mention. It has been argued by Patterson, among others, that the principle of "equality before the law" is at issue here; but it is difficult to see how the introduction of this principle clarifies or solves anything. For this principle, although doubtless commendable in the abstract, proves to have amazingly little content in concrete situations. What does it mean to say that people ought to be treated equally before the law? Does it mean that the only rules of law which are justifiable are those which apply indiscriminately to all persons? If so, then such a law is sufficiently rare as to be a curiosity. For almost every law, either explicitly or implicitly, makes exceptions for children, incompetents, sleepwalkers, and the like. In addition, almost all laws further circumscribe the class of persons who are to be treated in "equal" fashion by specifying the conditions that must be present before the law is to be applied. And here, too, very often these conditions include certain characteristics of possible litigants. For instance, there is generally one property law for good-faith purchasers and another for purchasers with notice; there may be one set of constitutional protections for aliens and another for citizens.

If, on the other hand, the principle of equality before the law imposes a weaker requirement upon justifiable laws—the requirement alluded to earlier that there be some reason for making the distinction made by the law—then appeal to the principle is simply not very helpful in any a priori fashion. Perhaps, for example, there is no good reason for making a rule which expressly recognizes that class of employees who have aided their employer, been injured, and subsequently received a promise of compensation from their grateful employer. Perhaps on balance such a "specialized" classification would be undesirable. But saying this is something quite different from asserting simply that the principle of "equality before the law" is necessarily violated whenever such a classification is made. Unless one is prepared to assert that all classifications, except those which include all human beings without exception, are inherently undesirable, an appeal to the principle of "equality before the law" is not by itself a forceful or convincing criticism of some "less inclusive" law. What must be shown is not the presence of a more selective classification, but rather the undesirability of making this kind of classification in this kind of case.

This does not mean that laws which make distinctions between persons on the basis of race, religion, place of origin, and the like cannot in most circumstances be condemned. This does not mean that laws which treat "equals unequally" are less abhorrent now than before. But it does mean that there may always be good reasons for making certain kinds of distinctions among persons. And it does mean that it is more appropriate to criticize the reasons offered than just to appeal to the principle of "equality before the law." The fact that a law discriminates among persons does not make the law bad; the fact that the law discriminates badly does. A "bad" law should be shown to be "bad" on this latter ground.

NONINTUITIVE EQUITY

In the course of the discussion so far, an equitable procedure has been defined as one that holds an intuition of the justness of a decision to be the necessary and sufficient justification for deciding a case in a certain fashion. It should be apparent, however, that those who have opposed equity to precedent have not limited their proposals solely to a demand for intuitive adjudication. Instead, much of what has been written about the desirability of equity has been written in praise of a procedure of justification in which precedents are not followed *and* in which intuition plays no role. Thus, even if intuition should be rejected as a criterion of justification—either for all cases or only for some—it does not follow that some other form of equitable justification must thereby be dismissed as unsatisfactory. In the remainder of this chapter the character of a nonintuitive equitable procedure will be presented very briefly; in the succeeding chapters it will be evaluated in considerably greater detail.

As has already been observed, the concept of an equitable procedure of justification rests very largely upon the notion that the peculiar or unique facts of each case ought to be taken into express account and given primary significance in order to do justice in the particular case. And there is at least one distinctly nonintuitive equitable procedure that would do just that. This nonintuitive equitable procedure stipulates that the court should concentrate upon the facts of a particular case, and should, after a "rational" consideration of all the facts, decide the case in such a way that justice is done for the litigants. Here, the rule of decision would prescribe that a decision is justifiable if and only if it best takes into account the interests of the litigants who are currently before the court. A decision is not justifiable because it is intuited to be such, or because it accords with some precedent. Rather, it is justifiable because the consequences of that decision are found to be more desirable for the litigants than those of any other possible decision. The interests of the litigants are primary; the consequences to them of deciding the case in one way rather than another are alone relevant to the question of what shall be regarded as a justifiable decision. If the courts consistently focus their attention upon the ways in which the litigants themselves will be affected by various possible decisions, and if the courts justify their decisions accordingly, then, it might be argued, they will render more justifiable decisions than they would were they to employ any other procedure of justification. Thus, this kind of nonintuitive equity would be embodied in a procedure in which courts justified their decisions solely on the basis of what decision would be best for the litigants.

A decision process such as this has considerable initial appeal. It does not seem to be open to the same criticisms which were made earlier of intuition as a criterion of justification. For under this form of an equitable procedure a judge could give perfectly good, independently verifiable reasons for deciding a case in a certain fashion. He could point to the way in which the decision would produce a minimum of discomfort and a maximum of satisfaction vis-à-vis the two litigants. He could receive evidence and analyze arguments that tended to show that one rather than another decision would be more justifiable on these grounds. Furthermore, such an equitable procedure would be free from many of the defects latent in a precedential procedure. Courts would not be bound by the errors of earlier procedure. They would be unhampered by tradition. They could meet each case as it came along and feel free to decide it and nothing more. This is, therefore, a procedure which surely requires careful study. And it may very well be the procedure which so many proponents of equitable adjudication have been implicitly suggesting all the time. Throughout the remainder of this work, I shall restrict the denotation of "equitable procedure" to a procedure which prescribes that cases ought to be decided in such a way as to bring about the best result as between the parties at present before the court. I shall assume that this is or can be a distinctly nonintuitive procedure.

At this juncture someone might object that, although the possibility of nonintuitive equitable procedures has been recognized, the discussion is still incomplete. For there is, the objection might continue, an additional and perhaps related theme which runs through almost all discussions of equity. It concerns the desirability of adjudicating either some or all cases by an appeal to moral rules or principles. Under this view, an equitable decision procedure is one in which courts are instructed to take moral rules or standards expressly into account and to employ these rules, rather than legal rules, as the criteria by which to justify particular decisions. Such a procedure could also be nonintuitive since moral rules can, arguably, be applied in the same fashion in which any other rules are applied. And the procedure could be nonprecedential, since an appeal to moral rules, rather than to already existing legal rules, constitutes the justification for deciding a case in a certain fashion.

This suggestion that cases ought to be decided in accordance with moral rather than legal rules is surely to be found in many of the writings to which reference has already been made. As usually formulated, however, its precise meaning is unclear. More specifically, there are at least two questions which must be resolved before it can even be considered as a possible, independent program of legal justification.

First, the *role* that moral rules or standards are to play in the process of justification must be delineated more precisely. Are the moral principles to function in the same manner in which legal rules function in a precedential decision procedure? If so, they would serve directly as the justification for a particular decision. Or are they to function instead as the criterion by which to evaluate particular legal rules? If so, they would not be the ostensible justification for particular decisions, but rather would be the justification for using a particular legal rule as the justification for a particular decision.

And second, the differences, if any, between moral and legal rules or principles must be examined more closely. Are there any formal differences between the two that would make it possible to say of any rule that if it is clearly a moral rule then it cannot be a legal rule, or if it is clearly a legal rule then it cannot be a moral rule? If a rule is a moral rule, does it follow that it cannot function in a procedure of justification in the same fashion in which a legal rule would function? If there is no inherent difference between the two kinds of rule, then is the suggestion that cases ought to be decided by an appeal to moral rules any different from the proposal that cases ought to be justified by reference to "new" or "alterable" legal rules? Is the suggestion that courts ought to be "equitable" any different from the proposal that courts ought to be free to change existing legal rules? Until these questions are answered, the possible significance of this second kind of nonintuitive equitable procedure cannot be fully understood. And once these questions are answered, as the questions themselves suggest, it may turn out that this is not even a distinctly equitable procedure at all.

Because almost all discussions of equity do invoke reference to adjudication in accordance with moral rules, and because this in turn can mean any one of several things, the following chapter constitutes something of a digression—although a necessary one—from the course of the argument so far. For in recent years, moral philosophers have been concerned with certain issues that have considerable relevance to a resolution of some of the problems just raised. In particular, they have sought to concern themselves with the role that the principle of utility ought to play in the justification of individual moral acts or decisions. The controversy that has been engendered over this point and the solutions that have been proposed are particularly useful in that they furnish instructive analogies to the possible roles which moral rules or principles—such as, for example, the principle of utility—might play in a procedure of legal justification.

6

Extreme and Restricted Utilitarianism

During the past fifteen years or so moral philosophers have spent much of their time debating the respective virtues of two kinds of utilitarianism. There are those who, calling themselves "restricted utilitarians," argue that many of the standard criticisms made of utilitarianism as a moral philosophy are misdirected because these criticisms have neglected the role that *moral rules* have had and ought to have in utilitarian moral justification. And there are those who, calling themselves "extreme utilitarians," argue that many of the standard criticisms of utilitarianism can be met more successfully if the additional difficulties that attend restricted utilitarianism are not introduced.[1]

As we shall see, there do not appear to be any formal points of disagreement between extreme and restricted utilitarianism—despite the fact that the merits of each have been urged as conclusive reasons for rejecting the other. There may, however, be certain practical differences between the two. Apart from the fact that a study of the nature of this controversy serves to introduce many of the issues involved in the question of the role that the principle of utility, and subsidiary rules, ought to play in a process of legal justification, there are two additional reasons for considering the recent philosophical debate. First, the restricted utilitarians have almost unanimously regarded the nature of the legal decision process as a singularly appropriate analogy for the schema of moral justification.[2] In effect, they have said, moral decisions ought to be justified in the same way in which legal decisions are justified; and further, the legal system does employ an essentially restricted utilitarian logic of justification. It is not within the scope of this inquiry to discuss whether the restricted utilitarians are correct in their understanding of the nature of legal justification. But it is surely relevant to consider the question, posed indirectly by the restricted utilitarians, of whether a procedure of legal justification analogous to that of restricted utilitarianism would be a desirable procedure of justification for the courts to employ. The restricted utilitarians may be wrong in thinking that the law is a good model for morals; but they may be correct in suggesting implicitly that restricted utilitarianism provides a fruitful model of the way in which legal justification ought to take place.[3]

The second reason for considering the controversy over these two moral theories *qua* moral theories is simply the fact that moral philosophers have tended to explore rather fully the nature and implications of these procedures of moral justification. If analogous procedures of legal justification deserve study, many of the observations of these philosophers may be instructive in a legal as well as a moral context.

RESTRICTED AND EXTREME UTILITARIANISM

The procedure of restricted moral justification can be quite simply delineated. If it is assumed that the "function" of morality is to encourage conduct that will produce a maximum of happiness or a minimum of conflict, then the highest-order ethical rule will be some formulation of the utilitarian principle. This, according to a theory of restricted utilitarianism, is the criterion by which particular moral *rules* are to be evaluated or justified. It is not the criterion (except in certain special cases not here relevant) by which the rightness of a particular *action* may be determined, since in such cases the only thing that is relevant is a particular moral rule. Thus, actions are to be justified by an appeal to moral rules, and moral rules are to be justified by an appeal to the principle of utility.

Although the essay is in no sense recent and although its author was a legal rather than a moral philosopher, one of the nicest formulations of the theory of restricted utilitarianism can be found in Lecture II of John Austin's *The Province of Jurisprudence De-*

termined. There, in answer to the objection that utilitarianism consists in the view that "if we adjusted our conduct to the principle of general utility, our conduct would always be determined by an immediate or direct resort to it," Austin offers the following argument:

Our conduct would conform to *rules* inferred from the tendencies of actions, but would not be determined by a direct resort to the principle of general utility. Utility would be the test of our conduct, ultimately, but not immediately: the immediate test of the rules to which our conduct would conform, but not the immediate test of specific or individual actions. Our rules would be fashioned on utility; our conduct, on our rules.

. . . .

If we would try the tendency of a specific or individual act, we must not contemplate the act as if it were single and insulated, but must look at the class of acts to which it belongs. We must suppose that acts of the class were generally done or omitted, and consider the probable effect upon the general happiness or good.

We must guess the consequences which would follow if acts of the class were general; and also the consequences which would follow if they were generally omitted. We must then compare the consequences on the positive and negative sides, and determine on which of the two the *balance* of advantage lies.

If it lie on the positive side, the tendency of the act is good: or (adopting a wider, yet exactly equivalent expression) the general happiness requires that *acts* of the *class* shall be done. If it lie on the negative side, the tendency of the act is bad: or (again adopting a wider, yet exactly equivalent expression) the general happiness requires that *acts* of the *class* shall be forborne.

In a breath, if we truly try the tendency of a specific or individual act, we try the tendency of the class to which that act belongs. The *particular* conclusion which we draw, with regard to the single act, implies a *general* conclusion embracing all similar acts.[4]

Phrased in a more contemporary philosophical idiom, the theory of restricted utilitarianism is a theory about two different kinds of moral reasons. There are reasons that are relevant to the criticism or justification of *individual actions* and there are reasons that are relevant to *social practices and rules.* If moral reasoning is to be properly understood, it must be realized that reasons which may be appropriate to the one are not necessarily appropriate to the other.

It was this distinction between the "reasons" for an individual action and the "reasons" for a social practice which Socrates made as he waited for the hemlock: he was ready to die rather than repudiate it—refusing, when given the chance, to escape from prison and so avoid execution. As an Athenian citizen, he saw that it was his duty (regardless of the actual consequences in his particular case) to respect the verdict and sentence of the court. To have escaped would have been to ignore this duty. By doing so, he would not merely have questioned the justice of the verdict in his case, he would have renounced the Athenian constitution and moral code as a whole. This he was not prepared to do.[5]

The theory of extreme utilitarianism can be stated equally succinctly. According to it, a particular moral act or decision is justifiable if and only if the particular consequences of an act are justifiable on utilitarian grounds. The desirability of extreme utilitarianism over restricted becomes obvious, it has been argued, once it is realized that a refusal to allow direct appeals to the principle of utility forces one to run the risk that a given action might turn out to be contrary to the principle of utility. This is not to insist that there may not be good reasons for regarding rules as appropriate rules of thumb in many instances. For example, the extreme utilitarian can recognize that often there is no time to calculate the consequential effects of a particular action. Similarly, the extreme utilitarian might know that "in particular cases where his own interests are involved his calculations are likely to be biased in his own favor. . . . [In such instances] he will probably come to the correct extreme utilitarian conclusion if he does not in this instance think as an extreme utilitarian but trusts to common sense morality."[6] But, it is argued, admitting all this,

is it not monstrous to suppose that if we *have* worked out the consequences and if we have perfect faith in the impartiality of our calculations, and if we *know* that in this instance to break [rule] R will have better results than to keep it, we should nevertheless obey the rule? Is it not to erect R into a sort of idol if we keep it when breaking it will prevent, say, some avoidable misery?[7]

The differences between these two kinds of utilitarianism emerge most dramatically, it is insisted, in the case of promise keeping. Suppose that someone has given me his gun to keep and I have promised to return it to him should he ask me for it. And suppose that after having talked several times about committing suicide, he comes to me in a particularly despondent mood and demands that I keep my promise by returning the gun to him immediately. It is argued that as an extreme utilitarian I might be justified in breaking my promise in this case on the grounds that the consequences of breaking my promise would in the long run be less deleterious than those which would result from honoring the promise and permitting an almost certain suicide. But as a restricted utilitarian, I would, arguably, be justified only in keeping my promise and returning the gun, because I had promised to do so and because the rule "Always keep your promises" is a rule which is clearly justifiable on utilitarian grounds.

On the basis of the description of these two procedures of moral justification, it is not difficult to see the form that two procedures of legal justification could take. Analogous to restricted utilitarianism would be a "two-level" logic of legal justification. Employing a two-level logic, a court would justify its decision in a particular case by appealing to some legal rule. Legal rules would, in other words, constitute the only appropriate justification for particular decisions. But the legal rule that is to be used to justify the particular decision would itself have to be justified on utilitarian grounds. Thus, in contrast to the model of precedent, the process of justification does not come to an end once the relevant rule of law has been located and applied. On the contrary, a legal rule is a valid justification for any particular decision if and only if that rule is itself justifiable on utilitarian grounds. And unlike the model of equity, legal rules do play a role in the process of justification. Considerations of justice or utility are relevant, but only to the evaluation of rules of law, not to the decision in a particular case.

Comparable to an extreme utilitarianism would be the procedure of legal justification in which the court justified its particular decisions by appealing directly to the principle of utility. The court might in many cases appeal to legal rules. But in every case it would be open to the court to decide whether in the given case more harm than good, on balance, would result from the application of the rule to the particular fact situation. And in every case the necessary and sufficient justification for a decision would consist in a finding by the court that in the long run *this* decision is more justifiable on utilitarian grounds than any other decision. Thus, in contrast to the model of precedent, it is not even a necessary condition that the court appeal to legal rules. And in contrast to the model of nonintuitive equity, it is not a sufficient condition that the interests of the litigants have been maximized.

To those who regard legal rules as an integral component of any legal system, the demand for a procedure of legal justification analogous to restricted utilitarianism—a two-level procedure of justification—strikes, no doubt, a responsive note. And to those who feel that an appeal to legal rules may just as often as not obstruct the giving of the decision that ought to be reached, the structure of an extreme utilitarian procedure of justification is probably more immediately attractive. But, as has already been suggested, whether there is any significant difference between these two procedures (as procedures of either moral or legal justification) is a question as yet unanswered. Before this question is faced directly, it will be desirable to consider the justifications which have been and which could be given for a restricted utilitarian procedure of justification. For, if there are no differences between the two procedures, the justifications for the one should be equally persuasive for the other. And if there are differences between extreme and restricted utilitarianism, the justifications for either ought to help to point up wherein the difference lies.

JUSTIFICATIONS FOR RESTRICTED UTILITARIANISM

Proponents of restricted utilitarianism have offered a plethora of cases, analogous to the case of Socrates referred to above, as illustrating the way in which the restricted theory would and does operate in many contexts. But an understanding of the manner in which a logic of "moral reasoning" or justification would function is at best only propaedeutic to the consideration of the critical question, i.e., whether such a logic is desirable. Indeed, if a theory analogous to restricted utilitarianism is to be offered as stating a desirable procedure of legal justification, it is necessary that the justifications of the ethical procedure be carefully explored. Unfortunately, contemporary moral theorists are less helpful at this

point. Despite the numerous examples of the way in which games
are played, rules of the road established, and hypothetical moral
arguments often conducted, there have been relatively few attempts to justify the employment of this logic as the procedure by
which moral actions ought to be evaluated. At least three kinds of
arguments have been urged in defense of restricted utilitarianism.
Yet only one of them seems to me to be at all persuasive as a justification either of a moral restricted utilitarianism or of a comparable procedure of legal justification.*

The Argument from Practice

One must look, the argument from practice insists, at the way
in which people reason about their ethical problems; one must
study the nature of ethical argument. When such an inquiry is
conducted, it is discovered that in cases in which there is a rule of
action that is both unambiguous and appropriate, the only reason
for having performed the action that is deemed proper is that the
action was required by the rule or practice. Most people justify
their moral conduct by appealing to the relevant moral rule: "there
is no more general 'reason' to be given beyond one which relates
the action in question to an accepted social practice."[8] If the rightness of the practice is called into question, then reasons of a different kind are considered appropriate, namely, those which justify
the practice *qua* practice on utilitarian grounds. It is simply of the
nature of moral reasoning as it usually occurs that "To question the
rightness of a particular action is one thing; to question the justice
of a practice as a practice is another." Another moral philosopher,

---

* In all fairness, however, it must be said that many of the exponents
of restricted utilitarianism may not have been seeking to give a justification
for restricted utilitarianism as a procedure of moral justification; they have
instead been trying only to analyze certain fairly typical moral arguments. If
this is so, they have not indicated this intention very clearly. More important,
at least some moral philosophers have apparently believed that moral arguments do not make any sense unless analyzed as being of a restricted utilitarian form. Such a view is certainly an implicit justification for restricted utilitarianism. Furthermore, the only question I am concerned with is whether
a restricted utilitarian form of justification would be a desirable one for the
courts to adopt. Thus, although I may be doing an injustice to the arguments
of some moral philosophers who have talked about restricted utilitarianism, I
am going to treat their remarks as speaking directly to the issue of whether
restricted utilitarianism is itself a desirable procedure of justification.

P. H. Nowell-Smith, has put the point this way:

To understand utilitarianism we must, therefore, distinguish questions about the reasons for adopting, retaining, or discarding a rule from questions about our obligation to obey the rule. The obligation to obey a rule does not, in the opinion of most ordinary men, rest on the beneficial consequences of obeying it in the particular case in either the short or the long run, as utilitarians have almost always supposed. But the reasons for adopting a rule may well be the kind that utilitarians suggest. It is, of course, impossible to prove that they are the only good reasons, since this would be a moral judgment. But it is a moral judgment that most men would be much more likely to endorse if it were not confused with the different moral judgment that we ought only to obey moral rules when the consequences of obedience are likely to be good.[9]

So far the argument is, conceivably, perfectly unobjectionable. This may very well be an accurate factual report of the way in which some people, or even many, happen to justify their moral decisions. For our purposes it is not necessary to discuss the question whether this is a correct *description* of ordinary moral argument (although I would add in passing that I do not think it is completely accurate). For even if it be conceded that a logic of this kind is the mode of ordinary ethical argument, it in no way follows that moral decisions ought to be justified on restricted utilitarian grounds. The argument from practice leaves the advocates of restricted utilitarianism open to the charge that they have confused an argument based upon what happens to be true with an argument founded upon what ought to be accepted. It is for a reason such as this that at least one critic of restricted utilitarianism, J. J. C. Smart, has repudiated this "milk and water" approach which describes itself sometimes as 'investigating what is implicit in the common moral consciousness' and sometimes as 'investigating how people ordinarily talk about morality.'" For, Smart insists, one need only "read the newspaper correspondence about capital punishment or about what should be done with Formosa to realize that the common moral consciousness is in part made up of superstitious elements, of morally bad elements, and of logically confused elements." What does it prove to say, as do both Toulmin and Nowell-Smith, that most men reason in this restricted fashion? Simply, that "it is more than likely that ordinary men are confused here."[10] The objection seems wholly sound.

The Linguistic Argument

Closely related to the argument from practice is the argument that rests the justification of restricted utilitarianist reasoning upon linguistic grounds. Here the point is not simply that some people reason in a restricted utilitarian fashion. Rather, the claim is made that this is the only way in which moral propositions and judgments make sense. Toulmin, for example, seems to rest his acceptance of restricted utilitarianism in part upon the thesis that the only way in which the question "Why ought I to do *x*?" can be intelligibly or meaningfully answered is to refer to the appropriate rule or practice.

Suppose that I say "I feel that I ought to take this book and give it back to Jones" (so reporting on my feelings). You may ask, "But ought you really to do so?" (turning the question into an ethical one), and it is up to me to produce my "reasons," if I have any. To begin with, then, I may reply that I ought to take it back to him "because I promised to let him have it back before midday." . . . "But ought you really?" you may repeat. If you do [I can reply] . . . "I ought to, because I promised to let him have it back." And if you continue to ask, "But why ought you really?" I can answer . . . "Because it was a promise." Beyond this point, however, the question cannot arise: there is no more general "reason" to be given beyond one which relates the action in question to an accepted social practice.[11]

John Rawls takes a similar position, arguing that rules define practice. That is, a particular act of, say, returning a book, can only be understood when seen to be in accordance with the rules that define the practice of promise keeping. For this reason, he asserts, it follows that

to engage in a practice, to perform these actions specified by the practice, means to follow the appropriate rules. . . . It doesn't make sense for a person to raise the question whether or not a rule or a practice correctly applies to *his* case where the action he contemplated is a form of action defined by a practice.[12]

The linguistic argument might be employed to make one of two points. In the first place, it might be introduced to establish the fact that many propositions can only have meaning within certain contexts—in relation to certain kinds of situations. For example, it would not make sense to justify a particular moral decision simply by appealing to the proposition that moral decision ought to be justified on a restricted utilitarian basis. It would not seem wholly intelligible for a person to respond to the question "Why ought I to return the book to Smith?" by simply asserting: "You ought to return the book to Smith because all moral decisions ought to be justified by appeal to a restricted utilitarian logic."

It is, furthermore, surely understood that the moral rule "One always ought to keep one's promises" is not a meaningful justification for the decision to help a needy stranger (assuming of course that whoever makes the decision has previously given no promise to help needy strangers).

If the linguistic argument were intended merely to demonstrate either or both of these points, it would be both unobjectionable and obvious. But in the hands of the advocates of a restricted utilitarian logic, it is introduced for quite another purpose. In particular, when used to support a restricted utilitarian mode of reasoning, the linguistic argument is understood to assert that the principle of utility can only be intelligibly employed as a justification for a rule; it insists that an attempt to justify a particular moral decision by a direct appeal to considerations of utility is literally meaningless. It is by no means obvious, however, that the principle of utility can only be intelligibly appealed to in a context of *rule justification.*

The problem could of course be made insignificant by a rephrasing of the principle of utility. The linguistic argument would be quite convincing if the principle of utility were stated as follows: "Rules of morality ought to minimize conflict and maximize satisfactions." Then it would be true that rules of morality alone, and not particular moral decisions, could be justified on utilitarian grounds. This would be so simply because the principle of utility has now been formulated in such a way as to make it relevant only to moral rules. But this begs the question at issue. The principle of utility as it is usually stated is not explicitly limited to the satisfactions and dissatisfactions which would be produced by a moral rule. It asserts rather that the criterion of all moral evaluation consists in a measurement of consequential happiness and discomfort. The restricted utilitarians are obviously seeking to demonstrate that a restricted utilitarian logic of justi-fication can best accomplish this end. They cannot, without beg-ging the question, show this simply by asserting that it does not make sense to apply the principle of utility to particular moral ac-tions, or—what comes to the same thing—by rephrasing the prin-ciple of utility so that it expressly does not apply to particular moral acts. This is the conclusion they wish to reach; it is not an argument that hastens their arrival.

It is perhaps nothing more than a restatement of what has al-ready been said to observe that the principle of utility does seem to be wholly intelligible when appealed to as a justification for a particular action. If, for example, the principle of utility states only that "One ought to act so as to maximize satisfactions and minimize conflict," then it seems to make perfectly good sense to ask of any particular moral action whether it in fact does maximize satisfactions and minimize conflicts. If someone were to announce that he planned to give all of his money to the United Nations Children's Fund because he believed this would be the way in which, all things considered, he could bring about the greatest amount of happiness with his money, his appeal to the principle of utility as the justification for his action is surely intelligible. Yet it is just this kind of appeal to utility which the linguistic argu-ment rejects as devoid of meaning.

At this point it is important to reiterate that many who put forward the above kind of argument for restricted utilitarianism are probably seeking to make a considerably weaker point. They are very likely suggesting not that a direct appeal to the principle of utility is unintelligible, but only that in many cases an appeal to some moral rule or practice is intelligible by itself—it does consti-tute a good reason for acting in a certain fashion. That is to say, the claim may be only that if, for example, one has made a promise to do something, the fact that one promised is a good reason for keeping the promise; no further reason is needed. What seems to be involved here is the suggestion that some kind of prima facie obligation arises, or some kind of prima facie justification exists, by virtue of the fact that the action in question is justifiable by an appeal to some accepted moral rule.

I think that as an analysis of such phenomena as promise keeping, and perhaps of other moral practices as well, this kind of analysis is probably correct. The "burden of proof" does seem to be placed quite properly upon the person who seeks to justify conduct which is not in accordance with an accepted moral rule. But to concede this still leaves open the question of what will turn this prima facie obligation into an absolute one. And here, if I understand restricted utilitarianism, the answer is this: A prima facie obligation, for example to keep one's promise, becomes absolute provided the moral rule in question, "Always keep your promises," is itself justifiable on utilitarian grounds. Thus, the fact that one promised to do something is, by itself, a good reason for doing it; and the fact that the rule "Always keep your promises" is a good rule makes the original good reason conclusive. It is this aspect of the restricted utilitarian logic of justification which must be explored more fully once the third justification for restricted utilitarianism has been considered.

There is, however, still another form of the linguistic argument which appears to have particular significance for legal decision procedures. It is suggested that utilitarianism makes most sense if what may be called the "judge's question" is kept separate from the "legislator's question."

The duty of the judge is to pronounce verdict and sentence in accordance with law; and the question "What verdict and sentence ought he to pronounce?" turns solely on the question "What verdict and sentence are laid down in the law for this crime?" As judge, he is not concerned with the consequences, beneficial or harmful, of what he pronounces. . . .
But the duty of the legislator is quite different. It is not to decide whether a particular application of the law is just or not, but to decide what laws ought to be adopted and what penalties are to be laid down for the breach of each law. . . . For if we interpret the legislator's question as one to be settled by asking "What does the law lay down for such a case?" we shall either be involved in an infinite regress, a hierarchy of laws in which the justice is determined by reference to a higher law, or we shall be forced to claim intuitive insight into a system of axiomatic laws, themselves requiring no justification, but providing the justification of all lower laws.[13]

I do not think that there is anything particularly wrong with statements of this kind, but it is also difficult to see how they go very far toward making a case for restricted utilitarianism. Assuming (what is clearly not the case) that there are no problems involved in deciding what a statute means or whether it applies to a particular case, then this only shows that the judge's question is really a trivial one. All of the interesting and significant problems are legislative problems. If this is the judge's question, he should have no difficulty in answering it in every case; indeed, it is hard to see why judges would be needed at all. Furthermore, as an analogy for moral justification, this example only shows that a person ought always to ask the legislator's question. A person ought always to ask "What rule would be the best rule for cases of this kind?" If the analogy suggests that a question comparable to the judge's question is an important moral question, if the analogy suggests that an action is morally just merely because it is in accordance with some existing moral rule, then it seems to be incorrect. Since in morals the same person ought to be both judge and legislator, since a person ought to ask whether the existing moral rule is a good rule, I do not see how the separation of the two questions adds anything of significance to the arguments for restricted utilitarianism.

In this connection, it is perhaps appropriate to add that it is for reasons of this kind that I have decided to talk about a legal system in which judges make as well as apply rules of law. I do not think that the judge's task ceases to be interesting once there are statutory legal rules. But I do think it is arguable, at least, that the judge's function is an essentially different one in these cases. There is doubtless a sense in which many of the things which I say about how cases ought to be decided are more applicable to legislatures than to courts of a code jurisdiction. But if, as so many legal philosophers have observed, judges can and should make law, and if, as even more legal philosophers have noted, the appeal to the common law is an appeal to rules of law made by judges in the past, then it is difficult to see why the "legislator's question" could not also be the "judge's question." Unless there are conclusive reasons for always following precedents, unless there are never cases which are not covered by a prior rule, and unless there are conclusive reasons for never altering an interpretation, once made, of a statute, then the way in which judges are to make and apply law poses meaningful and difficult questions. And it is to these questions that this work is addressed.

The Argument from Utility

In contradistinction to the two prior arguments, one justification for a restricted utilitarian logic is itself based upon utilitarian grounds. If I understand him correctly, John Rawls employs the argument from utility in his essay mentioned above.

There are, Rawls insists, utilitarian considerations which can justify a scheme of justification in which the only valid justification of a particular action is by appeal to the relevant rule. The point of many practices, he argues, may be precisely

to abdicate one's title to act in accordance with utilitarian and prudential considerations in order that the future may be tied down and plans coordinated in advance. There are obvious utilitarian advantages in having a practice which denies to the promisor, as a defense, any general appeal to the utilitarian principle in accordance with which the practice itself may be justified.

Practices are set up for various reasons, but one of them is that in many areas of conduct each person's deciding what to do on utilitarian grounds case by case leads to confusion, and that the attempt to coordinate behavior by trying to foresee how others will act is bound to fail.[14]

Thus, if I understand him correctly, Rawls's point is that there are *utilitarian* arguments which support the thesis that one ought not attempt to justify particular moral decisions by appealing directly to the utilitarian factors of those decisions. In other words, there may be a *utilitarian* justification for a moral decision procedure which does not itself consist in direct appeals to the principle of utility as a justification for particular decisions. When the merits of extreme and restricted utilitarianism are contrasted, so the argument runs, it is discovered that if a restricted utilitarianism is consistently employed, it will produce a greater quantum of particular decisions, themselves justifiable on utilitarian grounds, than will any other possible justificatory procedure. The point of the argument is this: If one is consistently a restricted utilitarian, then a greater number of particular results which are themselves justifiable on utilitarian grounds will be achieved than would be achieved were any other procedure of justification to be consistently employed.

This argument has considerable force and plausibility provided that we pay close attention to the requirements of the restricted utilitarian method of justification. For the question now is a purely empirical one—which justificatory procedure will produce the greatest quantum of desirable results? If someone is consistently an extreme utilitarian, will he end up doing more good acts than someone who is consistently a restricted utilitarian? Or will the converse be true? And what about a person who is sometimes a restricted utilitarian and sometimes an extreme utilitarian?

These questions can be best answered if the question of whether there is a real difference between being a restricted and an extreme utilitarian is confronted directly.

CAREFUL AND CARELESS UTILITARIANS

Consider more carefully the "second level" of the restricted utilitarian schema of justification—the insistence that the appeal to any particular moral rule or practice is justifiable if and only if the rule or practice is justifiable in the light of the principle of utility.

In general, restricted utilitarians have paid almost no attention to this second half of the restricted utilitarian thesis. Among other things, this failure to specify very precisely what it is they believe to be required by this second level of justification raises the following problem. The thesis is stated that the rule or practice to which particular decisions are to be appealed must itself be justifiable on utilitarian grounds. But what exactly does this mean? Does it mean, for example, that the rule in question if applied in all relevant cases would produce more justifiable results than any other rule or set of rules relating to the same subject matter? Or does it require only that the rule be not clearly unjustifiable? Consider the case of promise keeping. Everyone might agree that there is a sense in which the rule "Always keep your promises" is indeed justifiable on utilitarian grounds, that is, in the sense that it is surely more justifiable than the rule "Never keep your promises," or perhaps "Never keep your promises when it is not in your own self-interest to do so." And it is this kind of comparison that most restricted utilitarians seem to have had in mind when they have argued that a person ought to keep his promises because the rule "Always keep your promises" is justifiable on utilitarian grounds. It does not, however, seem at all obvious that because the rule "Always keep your promises" is more justifiable on utilitarian grounds than is some other rule concerning promise keeping, the rule "Always keep your promises" is necessarily the most justifiable rule (again on utilitarian grounds) which could be formulated concerning promise keeping. And it surely seems plausible to suppose that the requirement that the rule or practice be justifiable on utilitarian grounds means that the rule or practice must be the most justifiable rule or set of rules which can be devised for this kind of case. If this is so, the fact that the rule "Always keep your promises" is more justifiable than the rule "Never keep your promises" does not entail—even on restricted utilitarian grounds—that a particular decision to keep one's promise in a particular case is necessarily justifiable. For it might be the case that some other rule relating to promise keeping would be more justifiable on utilitarian grounds than the rule "Always keep your promises."

In the promise-keeping case presented earlier, it might turn out for instance that the rule "Always keep your promises except when keeping the promise would result very probably in the immediate loss of a human life" is more justifiable on utilitarian grounds than is the simpler rule. Thus it would be a mistake, if one were a careful restricted utilitarian, to be content to accept without examination the desirability of the rule "Always keep your promises." That rule is probably not as justifiable on utilitarian grounds as the more complicated rule involving the loss of life.

At this juncture it should be evident that the suggestions here advanced depend upon the arguments made in the preceding chapter concerning the universality and generality of rules.[15] For it is here argued that there is no formal difference between a rule which says "All promises ought to be kept," and one which says "All promises of a certain kind ought to be kept." The former rule is, of course, more general than the latter, but the two seem indistinguishable as rules in that each requires all members of the class specified by the rule to be treated in the same fashion.

Unless it can be shown that to make exceptions to a rule—in this sense of making exceptions—is different from making a new, more complicated rule or set of rules, it seems consistent with the tenets of restricted utilitarianism to interpret it as insisting that the rule or practice by which a particular action is to be justified must be the most justifiable rule or set of rules which at present seems capable of formulation. As a matter of fact, a much stronger thesis can be maintained: Unless restricted utilitarianism is interpreted as permitting the revision of the rule or practice whenever it can be demonstrated that the introduction of a new rule or practice is more justifiable on utilitarian grounds, it does not seem at all obvious that restricted utilitarianism has much to commend it. In particular, it no longer seems very plausible to suppose that restricted utilitarianism could, as a matter of fact, be justified on utilitarian grounds, simply because it now seems doubtful that a system of justification which prevented the alteration of rules under any conditions could provide a greater quantum of justifiable results than some alternative justificatory procedure which did permit revision of the rules. But if, on the contrary, restricted utilitarianism does permit a new rule to be substituted whenever the introduction of that rule can be shown to yield a greater quantum of justifiable results than the retention of the extant rule, then it seems that restricted utilitarianism can indeed be defended upon empirical grounds.

But now a rather curious situation develops. It appears that some new rule, more justifiable on utilitarian grounds, could be introduced in many, if not all, of those cases in which the results of extreme and restricted utilitarianism appeared to conflict. For it is those cases in which the application of the extant rule to the particular case would produce a result that is unjustifiable on extreme utilitarian grounds which suggest that there is something wrong with the extant rule and, therefore, that some new and better rule which takes special account of this kind of case could probably be devised.[16] If this is so, it is difficult to detect any important theoretical distinctions between extreme and restricted utilitarianism. If the rules to which particular acts are to be appealed are themselves to be revised upon a showing that the new proposed rule or set of rules is more justifiable on utilitarian grounds, and if there is no theoretical limitation upon the number of rules which can be introduced, then it is hard to envision a case in which the restricted utilitarian would *necessarily* be compelled to reach a result different from that reached by an extreme utilitarian. And, on the other hand, if restricted utilitarianism does not permit the introduction of a new rule or set of rules whenever it can be shown that the introduction of this new rule or set of rules is more justifiable on utilitarian grounds than the preservation of the old rule, then it is extremely difficult to see how a case could be made out for the proposition that restricted utilitarianism would produce a greater quantum of justifiable results than would a careful extreme utilitarianism. Unless there are independent reasons for adopting an essentially conservative position in regard to moral rules, customs, and practices, a restricted utilitarianism that does not permit the revisability of rules seems little better than an uncritical acceptance of the moral and social status quo. And yet, if revisability is permitted within restricted utilitarianism, the formal distinctions between it and extreme utilitarianism are rendered insignificant, if not nonexistent. If an extreme utilitarian is careless, he may very well neglect just those long-term considerations which a restricted utilitarian would never overlook. If a restricted utilitarian is careless, he may very well forget than even usually accepted rules are always open to question. But if each is careful in employing his procedure of justification, it is hard to envision a case in which moral disagreement would be inevitable.

Granted all this, there are still two things which can be said in defense of restricted utilitarianism as a separate doctrine. In the first place, restricted utilitarianism performs the practical function of forcing concentration upon the kinds of consequences that should always be taken into account and that all too often are apt

to be neglected. By focusing upon the justifiability of rules, restricted utilitarianism requires the explicit consideration of the
long-term consequences of acting in various ways. It points up the
fact that, for example, decisions to act in a certain way may have
an effect upon the way in which others will act in the future. It
calls attention to the fact that one of the consequences of, say,
breaking a promise is that others may not retain much faith in
future promises. As I understand the position of extreme utilitarianism, a *careful* extreme utilitarian would also take these considerations into account. But perhaps a restricted utilitarian would
be more easily led to regard considerations of this kind as necessarily relevant. If one is a careful extreme utilitarian, one should
find the same actions justifiable that a careful restricted utilitarian
would regard as justifiable. But perhaps one is more apt to be a
careless extreme utilitarian than a careless restricted utilitarian.

And, in the second place, restricted utilitarianism expressly
leaves open the possibility that there may be classes of cases in
which a rule that is relatively free from exceptions and not readily
open to revision might be the best rule to follow in all cases. I do
not see how one could say, a priori, that all or even some particular
rules ought to be of this kind, but it does seem to me to be possible
for a restricted utilitarian to show that a particular rule which was
never subject to revision might produce a greater quantum of justifiable results than would any other rule.

In the succeeding chapter a procedure of legal justification that
is analogous to that of a careful restricted utilitarian is considered
in detail. It is a two-level procedure of legal justification in which
courts are to justify their decisions by appealing to legal rules, and
in which they are to justify these legal rules by appealing to the
principle of utility. For the reasons just given, I do not believe
there are any formal differences between such a procedure and one
which would be analogous to a careful extreme utilitarianism—one
in which courts justified their decisions by appealing the long-term
consequences of deciding the case in a certain way directly to the
principle of utility. I do think, however, that there are some practical differences of the kinds just alluded to, between a restricted
and an extreme utilitarian "orientation." And I am even more con-

vinced that there are differences of a most radical sort between a careful restricted utilitarianism and the kind of nonintuitive equitable procedure delineated at the end of the preceding chapter. Irrespective of the practical significance of being a restricted rather than an extreme utilitarian, it is theoretically as well as practically of great significance to be either a restricted or an extreme utilitarian rather than an "equitable utilitarian." For to hold, as does the equitable procedure, that a decision is justifiable if and only if it maximizes the satisfactions of the litigants before the court, is to propose a procedure of justification which is markedly different in kind from one which insists that, at the very least, there are other kinds of considerations which must be taken into account before a decision is to be deemed justifiable. It is to the explication of these differences that the following chapter is devoted.

7

The Two-Level Procedure of Justification

In the concluding section of Chapter 5 the characteristics of a nonintuitive equitable decision procedure were delineated but not evaluated. That procedure had as its rule of decision the rule which prescribes that a decision is justifiable if and only if the consequences of that decision to the litigants are found to be more desirable, on balance, than the consequences of any other decision. In the previous chapter the nature of a two-level procedure of justification, the analogue of a careful restricted utilitarianism, was described. That procedure has as its rule of decision the rule which prescribes that a decision is justifiable if and only if it is deducible from the legal rule whose introduction and employment can be shown to be more desirable than any other possible rule. This chapter examines the kinds of decisions that would be held to be justifiable under each of these two procedures.

It is essential that the point at issue in this comparison be made clear at the outset. What are to be contrasted are the decisions that would be forthcoming were one or the other of these two procedures of justification to be unequivocally employed by the judiciary. Thus the question is not which procedure would permit of a more desirable decision in any particular case, but rather which procedure, if consistently invoked, would regard as justifiable more desirable decisions than the other. The two-level procedure of justification can be shown to be superior to the equitable procedure only if it can be demonstrated that the practice of deciding cases in accordance with the equitable rule of decision would produce a set of decisions less desirable than the set that would be rendered were the two-level procedure to be employed. Conversely, the equitable procedure can be shown to be superior to the two-level procedure only if the set of decisions forthcoming under the two-level procedure would be less desirable than the set of decisions justifiable under the equitable rule of decision. What will be compared, in other words, are the consequences of regarding these two different procedures as furnishing the criteria for selecting the reasons which are to be accepted as conclusively good reasons for deciding a case in a certain fashion.

The arguments in this chapter demonstrate fairly convincingly, it is submitted, that the two-level procedure would be more desirable than the equitable one. But they do not, unfortunately, show the two-level procedure to be wholly free from difficulties of its own. To select only one of the more serious problems: a curious paradox pervades the entire discussion of the procedure. Many of the virtues of the two-level procedure stem from the fact that legal *rules* play such a significant role in the justification of individual decisions. Yet, in the light of what was said in the preceding chapter, the two-level procedure of justification is theoretically indistinguishable from the analogue of a careful extreme utilitarianism—a procedure which would require each decision to be justified by a consideration of all the significant consequences, long-term and short-term, of deciding the case in that fashion. And here, justification is possible without recourse to rules at all. Consequently, although the desirability of the two-level procedure depends in part upon its insistence that decisions be justified by an appeal to appropriate legal rules, this requirement does not seem *necessary* to the formulation of the rule of decision.

In this chapter we shall first consider the three respects in which the equitable and two-level procedures may be contrasted. These are: (1) the effect of the procedure upon the class that the decision seeks to protect; (2) the significance of the procedure in cases in which knowledge of probable legal consequences was not present; and (3) the restrictions placed by the procedure upon the kinds of evidence relevant to a reasoned justification of a decision. Second, explicit attention will be paid to certain objections, not previously described, which might be made to the two-level procedure. In particular, two questions are considered, although not in great detail: (1) Is the requirement of two levels of justification substantively as well as formalistically significant? (2) Can the two-level procedure be helpful in the adjudication of cases in which the court ought to employ its discretion or invoke the aid of some general standard?

THE TWO-LEVEL AND EQUITABLE PROCEDURES COMPARED

The Direct Effect of Decisions upon the Class to be Protected

On the surface it would seem that the two-level procedure would be invoked most appropriately in those cases in which it is essential that there be a legal rule and in which the content of the legal rule is relatively unimportant. Such things as the familiar rules of the road, the rules for the effective time of an offer or an acceptance of a contract, and the rules of domicile for conflict-of-laws purposes come immediately to mind. But for the reasons already stated in connection with the discussion of Roscoe Pound's bifurcation theory of equity, it is evident that such an argument cannot rest upon the grounds usually advanced. For even those rules which themselves lack any significant moral content may have strikingly immoral consequences when applied in particular contexts. Even in the areas in which the need for a settled rule seems greatest, the application of that rule to the parties before the court may produce seemingly disastrous results. The proponents of an equitable decision procedure can quite properly point out that in any area of the law, the most unobjectionable law can have the most obnoxious consequences. The most obviously "neutral" law of property may have shockingly deleterious effects when applied to a lessor who cannot vacate the premises because his mother is seriously ill. The most innocuous rule pertaining to the foreclosure of mortgages may, if invoked against a poor widow, lead to incalculable harm to the widow and those dependent upon her. The proponents of an equitable decision procedure can point to circumstances such as these and can insist with considerable persuasiveness that the courts can best perform their function if they abstain from using rules of law at all and concentrate instead upon doing justice in the case currently before the court. Thus, if a rule-applying procedure is to be shown to be more desirable than an equitable procedure, reasons in addition to those usually alleged must be advanced.

Such reasons can be found. For consider more closely the typical fact situation in which the case for an equitable decision procedure seems strongest. Consider the typical hardship case—that of the poor mortgagor and the wealthy mortgagee. Imagine the plight of Widow Jones, who lives with her six children on an old and heavily mortgaged farm. It is winter and perhaps a light snow has begun to fall. The date upon which the mortgage payment was due has come and gone. Bachelor Smith, already the richest man in town, holds the mortgage on the land. He goes into court seeking an order which would foreclose the mortgage and evict the widow. What decision would a court be justified in giving?

If an equitable logic of justification is adopted, it is evident, no doubt, that more harm than satisfaction would on balance result from a decision which allowed the mortgage to be foreclosed and the widow and her children forced out, homeless, into the snow. Bachelor Smith admittedly has no need for the land or for the money that might be realized from its sale. Widow Jones has no place else to live. Considering merely the respective positions of the parties before the court, it would be a heartless and inhuman judge who would fail to see that a consideration of the interests, needs, and potential satisfactions of the litigants required him to prevent the mortgagee from evicting the widow.

But appealing as this argument may be, it is difficult to see how such a *decision procedure* could be defended. In essence, the equitable judge would be saying that a mortgage should not be foreclosed whenever considerably more pain would result to the mortgagor than satisfaction to the mortgagee. And it is this which cannot by itself be sustained as a sufficient justification for the decision. For is it not reasonable to suppose that one of the significant consequences of deciding mortgage cases in this way would be that persons who were most in financial need and who were most likely to remain in financial need would be unable to borrow money from prospective creditors? The practice of adjudicating mortgage cases on this basis might have the effect, therefore, of destroying the utility of those security devices upon which mortgage transactions depend. Potential creditors might quite understandably be reluctant to lend money to those persons who probably would be hurt most by forfeiture of the mortgaged property in case of default. Thus, those who were most in need of some device by which they could borrow money would probably be unable to find willing lenders. And it would probably follow, too, that those who were best able to lend money, i.e., those with the least need, would be least likely to do so simply because there would be a greater probability that their interest would be overridden in any particular judicial conflict.[1] Consequently, conceding that the institution of capitalism and its credit devices are economically desirable, the employment of a logic of justification based solely upon equitable considerations would tend to defeat the very purposes of those institutional devices. If it is admitted that credit transactions are desirable, then it becomes evident that something more than a consideration of the effect of the decision upon the litigants before the court is a necessity if these transactions are to continue to be made in the future.

Adjudication in accordance with a two-level procedure of justification would do just that. Conceding the importance of permitting impecunious borrowers to borrow money from lenders, and of encouraging wealthy lenders to lend the money, some rule of law that effects a balance between the potential risk and security to the creditor must be formulated and applied by the courts. Utilitarian considerations are surely crucial to the formulation of the most desirable rule of mortgage law. But for the reasons outlined above, they will surely be neglected if only the interests of the parties before the court are considered. The practice of deciding particular mortgage cases by considering only the consequences of the decision to the litigants is more likely to result in undesirable consequences of a more serious and far-reaching nature than is the practice of deciding particular cases by an appeal to that legal rule which on utilitarian grounds is deemed most desirable.

Such a formulation of the problem, although correct, is likely to be misleading in one respect. The delineation is useful in so far as it calls attention to the fact that strikingly deleterious consequences will, arguably, flow from the adoption of an equitable decision procedure. The statement is proper, too, in an implicit insistence that what must be found within any justification for a particular mortgage decision is a consideration of the long-term effect of deciding this and comparable mortgage cases in a certain fashion. The formulation is misleading, however, if it gives the impression that the rule which is to be formulated could not be revised under any circumstances. And it is misleading if it suggests that a rule which took special account of widows would necessarily be unacceptable.

For the point of objecting to the equitable utilitarian justification is not—as some might think—that the equitable procedure takes widows into account while a two-level decision procedure does not. It does not follow that within the two-level procedure there cannot be a rule of mortgage law which treats mortgages in which widows are mortgagors as a special class. The point of objecting to the equitable procedure is simply that it cannot take widows into account in the way it should. If courts justify their decisions not to enforce mortgages against widows on the grounds that more harm will accrue to the widow than satisfaction to the mortgagee, the courts will, arguably, in the long run hurt more widows more severely than would be the case if they enforced at least some kinds of mortgages against even destitute widows. There is, it should be repeated, nothing necessarily incompatible between a two-level decision procedure and a special rule of mortgages for widows. The two-level procedure only requires, in a fashion in which the equitable procedure cannot, that there should be a rule for widows only if it can be shown that the singling out of widows for special treatment will not in the long run do more harm than good to widows. By insisting that the long-term effects of treating widows in a certain fashion be made relevant to the way in which any particular case involving a widow is to be decided, the two-level procedure is in fact the only procedure which can take the presence of widows into account in any very meaningful fashion.

Furthermore, even if it could be shown that some special rule of mortgage law which took widows into account would not be "self-defeating" vis-à-vis the interests of widows, there might still be other reasons that would militate against the introduction of the rule. But since such considerations speak to the question of what kinds of legal rules ought to be employed rather than to the question of whether legal rules ought to be employed at all, discussion of these matters is postponed until the differences between an equitable and a two-level procedure of justification have been more fully explored.[2]

Now, someone might agree that employing an equitable decision procedure would be "self-defeating" in this kind of case, without assenting to the proposition that a two-level logic of justification ought to be employed as the procedure by which to justify all legal decisions. Indeed, the proponent of an equitable procedure might argue along the following lines: "The mortgage case just discussed only indicates that there is obviously a sense in which people's actions are going to be based upon their understanding of the way in which the legal system will probably treat these actions. By employing a two-level procedure of justification, a judge is able to take this factor into account in a way in which he could not were he to use an equitable procedure. There are obviously many areas of the law, other than that of mortgages, in which adherence to an equitable decision procedure would in the long run lead to extremely unfortunate results. People would probably not make many of the kinds of contracts that they certainly ought to be encouraged to make, if they thought that the courts would adjudicate particular contractual disputes by deciding which of the two parties would be the more severely injured by a decision adverse to his claim. And the same can doubtless be said for many of the most important and socially desirable forms of property transactions.

"But even granting all this, is it still not true that there exists a large—in fact a very large—class of cases in which people never use their knowledge of legal consequences as controlling guides for action? What about those cases in which a knowledge of how the court has regarded similar cases in the past or is apt to regard similar cases in the future, has no effect upon the actions undertaken by an individual? The two-level procedure of justification does not appear to make much sense when applied, for example, to the hardship case discussed earlier—the case in which the employee saved his employer from injury only at the cost of injuring himself.[3] Would it not be fantastic to suppose that his action was influenced in any way by the knowledge that if his employer would subsequently offer to compensate him for his injuries, this promise would be given effect? Would it not be chimerical to assume that other employees might be induced to save their employers from injury if they knew of the existence of a rule such as that invoked in the *Webb* case? And would it not be equally absurd to believe that grateful employers will be deterred from promising to compensate their employees if they know that the courts will use an equitable procedure to adjudicate particular cases of this kind? Can it be shown, in other words, that a consideration of anything more than the interests of the parties before the court is needed in order to reach good decisions, even long-run good decisions, in cases of this kind?

"Or, to take a different example, consider the following case. John Hawkins, a man of dubious moral character, met a girl of seventeen who was working as a waitress in a night spot in Oklahoma. Her virtue is also highly suspect since that same night she agreed to go with him across the border into another state. Furthermore, she was taken by Hawkins with the understanding, apparently, that she would live with his common-law wife, who was a prostitute. There, under the wife's tutelage, the young girl was to learn and to employ the secrets of putatively the oldest of all professions.

"Hawkins was indicted for violation of the Mann Act and brought to trial in one of the Federal district courts. For reasons not now relevant it became evident that the testimony of Hawkins's wife was crucial to the case for the government. But there was a problem whether such testimony was admissible. It was, arguably, the rule in the Federal courts that—with the exception of a very limited number of crimes—testimony adverse to a defendant by a defendant's wife or husband was inadmissible in criminal prosecutions, even if the spouse were willing to give the needed evidence. The wife's testimony having been permitted by the trial court, appeal on this point was taken by Hawkins to the Supreme Court.

"On appeal, a unanimous court held (one judge concurring only in the result) that the rule concerning the admissibility of such testimony ought not to be changed, and that therefore the testimony in this case was improperly permitted.[4] The rule that one spouse should never be allowed to testify against the other in criminal cases rests, said the court, speaking through Mr. Justice Black, on the desire to foster peace in the family. 'The basic reason the law has refused to pit wife against husband or husband against wife in a trial where life or liberty is at stake was a belief that such a policy was necessary to foster family peace, not only for the benefit of husband, wife and children, but for the benefit of the public as well. Such a belief has never been unreasonable and is not now.'[5] Since this rule is a good rule, said the court, sounding just like the advocates of a two-level procedure, it ought to be applied in this case.

"Now, is it not wholly unrealistic to suppose that Hawkins was in any way influenced by an awareness of the fact that his wife would be unable to testify against him should he be indicted under the Mann Act? Furthermore, even if he knew of the rule, does it necessarily follow that the same kind of socially harmful consequences as were envisioned in the mortgage case would result if the court were to decide cases like the *Hawkins* case on equitable grounds? How, for example, would the practice of deciding in a particular case whether one spouse should be permitted to testify against the other obviously tend to weaken the institution of marriage? In particular, since in the instant case the court was faced with a marriage in which the wife was a prostitute and the husband a procurer, were not the conditions necessary for domestic peace lacking from the outset? Why, granted the circumstances, should the exclusionary rule nevertheless have been applied? Why, in other words, should the mere fact that the exclusionary rule is generally defensible be a good and sufficient reason for applying the rule in every case regardless of the result in any particular case? Why should questions of the peculiar merits of the instant case be disregarded? And why, even if a two-level procedure of justification is employed, should not the court have formulated a new rule or set of rules that would exclude the testimony of prostitutes, for example, from the scope of the questioned rule of evidence? In short, was not the only result of applying this rule of evidence in this case to allow a socially undesirable character—one who makes his living from trading in commercialized vice—to escape the sanctions of a statute which was clearly enacted to prevent this kind of activity by punishing all such offenders?

"It would seem to follow, therefore, that although there may be some areas of the law in which a two-level procedure of justification is desirable, there are also other areas in which the argument for it simply does not apply. And it would appear to follow, further, that the more sensible approach would consist in deciding cases of this latter kind directly on their merits."

It should be observed that an argument such as this one can be construed as suggesting at least two different things. On the one hand, the argument might be proposing that there are no very good reasons why an equitable decision procedure ought not to be employed to decide questions comparable to those present in the *Webb* and *Hawkins* cases. It might, that is, be urging that in cases of this kind, the judge ought to consider each marriage, or each employer and employee, as litigation arises, and decide which of the parties would be hurt least and benefited most by the decision. And it is this determination which ought to serve as the justification for the decision. On the other hand, the argument might be directed toward the thesis that the legal rule which is usually employed to decide cases of this kind is not necessarily the best legal rule that could be formulated. The rule granting a general husband-wife privilege is not, perhaps, the best rule of evidence that could be devised; a more complicated rule which makes an exception for prostitute-procurer marriages ought to have been introduced as the justification for permitting Hawkins's wife to testify. The general rule of contracts ought to be revised in such a way that certain kinds of past or moral considerations are expressly permitted to support a future promise to pay money.

It should be apparent that the first of these two interpretations raises the question of whether an equitable procedure is more desirable, at least in some kinds of cases, than a two-level procedure. The second interpretation raises the question of whether the two-level procedure was employed in a satisfactory manner, and it perhaps, at least implicitly, raises the question of whether the two-level procedure is apt to lead courts to accept uncritically existing rules of law as the sufficient justification for their decisions. But it is one thing to suggest that an equitable procedure ought to be adopted and quite another to suggest that the two-level procedure may be misemployed. While these are both points that require discussion, they are best kept separate.

Construed as a defense of the use of the equitable decision procedure (in at least some kinds of cases) the lengthy argument suggested above is persuasive in its insistence that the same kind of justification for a two-level decision procedure cannot be invoked in all cases. It must be conceded, for example, that were cases involving the admissibility of the testimony of a spouse to be decided on equitable grounds, the same kinds of "self-defeating" consequences found in the mortgage cases would not necessarily occur. People might still get married with the same frequency even if they knew that were the question to arise, a court would evaluate their particular marriage in order to determine whether one spouse ought to be permitted to testify against the other. But to allow this much is not to concede the desirability of an equitable decision procedure even in cases of this kind. To admit that people often act without a knowledge of the probable legal consequences, and to admit further that a knowledge of the probable legal consequences is just as often not an influential factor upon their actions, is not to concede that the two-level procedure ought not to be employed here. On the contrary, there are two other arguments that support an adherence to a two-level rather than an equitable procedure of justification—even in cases like the *Hawkins* case.

Action Taken Without a Knowledge of Probable Legal Consequences

It is certainly true that people often act without being aware of the probable legal consequences of their actions, but this does not necessarily imply that the opportunity to so consider these consequences ought not to be made available to them. Provided that there is agreement with what was said earlier concerning the desirability of predictability,[6] it would follow that the legal system ought always to seek to increase the areas in which anticipation of the legal consequences of action will be possible. If this is so, the mere fact that people do not act upon a consideration of the legal effects of their action does not imply that rules of law on which they can intelligently rely are superfluous.

Concomitantly, there does not seem to be any area of the law in which it is not essential for lawyers to be able to predict the result of litigation. Even if a lawyer's client was not influenced in his activity by a knowledge of the law, it is important that the lawyer be able to ascertain the way in which the court will regard this activity. For if the lawyer can make a plausible prediction concerning the judicial result, he can decide more intelligently such things as whether the controversy should be litigated, or whether, instead, some out-of-court settlement ought to be sought.

If the argument to this point is convincing, the question that must be asked is: Which of the two decision procedures—the equitable or the two-level—is better able to provide the conditions for antecedent knowledge? Here the two-level procedure may be more efficacious. For consider the way in which an equitable decision procedure would operate. To begin with, the factors which in any particular case will be relevant to a decision will very often not be ascertainable until the moment of litigation arrives. If the rule of decision is to be understood to require that the interests and needs of the litigants before the court must be considered, then a determination of what decision would be so justifiable cannot be effected until the characteristics of the particular litigants are known. For example, a court operating under such a decision procedure ought to take into account such things as the relative wealth, ages, sensibilities, and potentialities of the parties actually involved in the litigation. For these factors are all relevant to the question of what decision would maximize satisfaction between the two litigants; these are also often unascertainable prior to the fact of litigation, and prior to the time at which the litigants become known to one another.

If, on the contrary, a two-level logic of justification is unequivocally employed by the judiciary, the conditions necessary for accurate prediction are more obviously present. All that was said in Chapter 4 concerning the degree to which a decision procedure based upon the rule of decision of stare decisis can make prediction possible is equally relevant here. Precisely because particular cases are to be justified by an appeal to the appropriate legal rule, there is a better opportunity to predict correctly under which rule litigation will fall and what legal consequences will attach.

There is, however, an obvious objection to this suggestion that predictability will be easier under the two-level procedure. For the two-level procedure differs from precedent precisely in the respect that the two-level procedure permits existing rules of law to be altered under certain conditions. Because the two-level procedure permits—and in fact requires—legal rules to be altered whenever there is a new, more desirable, legal rule, it does not seem that predictions will be any more accurate here than under the equitable procedure. Indeed, the two-level logic of justification was expressly stipulated to be analogous to a *careful* restricted utilitarianism in order to avoid confusing existing legal rules with truly justifiable ones. And once it is admitted, as it must be, that legal rules can and should be revised by the court whenever the introduction of a new rule can be shown to be more justifiable, then the similarity between the two-level procedure and a precedential one seems to disappear. It is surely possible under the two-level procedure that the rule of law which was used by the parties (or either party) as the basis for prediction may be rejected by the court as a now undesirable rule when the case comes up for adjudication. Here, then, is one of the dilemmas that seems unavoidable. If there are no legal rules upon which people can rely, society loses something of real significance. If there are to be rules of law which can be safely relied upon, then these rules ought to be unalterable. But neither alternative is satisfactory. The two-level procedure, although far from being a perfect solution to this problem, is perhaps the best one achievable.

For there are two factors that make it plausible to suppose that a considerable degree of predictability may be possible within the two-level procedure. First, once a rule of law has been formulated and adjudged to be a desirable rule of law, it is relatively unlikely that circumstances which would upset the correctness of the judgment will be present in the near future. If it is supposed, for instance, that a desirable rule of mortgage law has been derived, the conditions that make this a desirable rule are not apt to be altered either very suddenly or very often.[7] Although it is always open to a litigant to show that some other rule would be more desirable than the existing rule, the burden would be upon that litigant to show precisely how the judgment of the existing rule's desirability is now incorrect.

And second, while the two-level procedure of justification may not be able to "guarantee" that a case will be decided in accordance with the existing rule, it does succeed in focusing the attention of the judge upon the fact that the *introduction* of the new rule must be justifiable (as well as the content of the new rule itself) before the new rule ought to be counted a conclusively good reason for deciding a case in accordance with that rule.

In this connection, too, the two-level procedure would clearly not preclude a court from deciding that some new rule ought to be applied only in fact situations arising subsequent to the announcement of the new rule. That is to say, once it is conceded that existing legal rules ought to be changed, it does not follow that the only possible course is to apply the new rule to the case then before the court. If the old rule is the kind of rule that the litigants probably relied upon, it may be more desirable to apply the old rule to this case, while announcing that future activity ought to be based upon the new rule.[8] There are surely times when such an approach would be more sensible than one that either automatically applies the new, more desirable, rule to all cases or absolutely refuses to alter the existing rule on the grounds that people have relied upon it.[9] Thus, while the two-level procedure explicitly stipulates that existing legal rules may be changed, it allows the consequences of overruling to be taken into account. And it permits, as well, the force of that revision to have a variety of effects.

The two-level procedure cannot provide the degree of predictability that might, in the abstract, be more desirable. But it does seem to be able to take into account, in a way in which the equitable procedure cannot, the issues necessarily involved in providing predictability. And it does, at the same time, seem to be able to take into account, in a way in which the precedential procedure cannot, the issues necessarily involved in having desirable laws.

Activity for Which a Knowledge of Legal Consequences Is Unimportant: The Two Kinds of Evidence

"All the arguments that have been presented so far," the advocate of an equitable procedure might still respond, "have shown at most that a two-level procedure is most desirable in those areas of the law in which people either can predict or ought to be able to predict the legal consequences of actions. There still remains, however, a large area in which the possibility of prediction is simply not an important goal and in which adherence to a two-level procedure could only result in doing injustice in particular cases. A knowledge of all the relevant rules of law might not, for example, have the slightest effect upon the number or kinds of 'crimes of passion' that are committed daily. Furthermore, there are many more cases in which the arguments already advanced, while relevant, are simply not persuasive. In the *Hawkins* case, for instance: regardless of what Hawkins may or may not have known about the husband-wife exclusionary privilege, it seems silly to have applied that rule of evidence in his case. Husbands and wives in general will surely not be upset—marriage as an institution will not be weakened—if Hawkins's common-law wife, a prostitute, had been permitted to testify to his socially reprehensible acts. And the point is not simply that a new, more complicated rule of evidence ought to have been formulated. The point is rather that in cases of this kind there does not seem to be any good reason why the judge simply should not decide the cases on a 'case by case' basis. There is nothing to be gained by formulating rules of law; there are not even any obvious long-term consequences in deciding the case one way or the other. What has simply got to be decided by the judge is whether in this particular case the possible preservation of Hawkins's marriage—if one can call it that—is more important than sending a socially vicious corrupter of youth to jail under a rule that was specifically intended to punish individuals like him. If the interest Hawkins has in *his* marriage had been weighed against the interest of the state in removing him at least temporarily from society, it is plain that the interest of the state should have prevailed here."

This argument, while perhaps overdrawn, introduces for discussion the last of the three major arguments for the desirability of a two-level procedure of justification over an equitable one. For even if it is conceded that neither of the two preceding arguments applies to a case like the *Hawkins* case, there is another one which in a sense is the most inclusive of the three. For this argument applies not only to cases like the *Hawkins* case but to any case at all that might come before the courts for adjudication. It relates to the nature of the inquiry that would be conducted by the court; it relates to the character of the evidence that would be deemed relevant under the two different procedures.

Consider first the kind of evidence that in an equitable procedure of justification would be relevant to the question of whether Mrs. Hawkins should be allowed to testify. The judge would have to make a rather detailed investigation of the particular marital life of the parties before the court. He would have to have information about their particular feelings toward one another. On this basis he would have to form a judgment as to the probable result of permitting Mrs. Hawkins to testify. He would, in other words, have to predict the likelihood of her testimony's causing a permanent breach in their relationship. He would, further, be forced to evaluate the benefit to society of preserving this particular marriage. And finally, he would have to decide whether the possible pain that might result from the dissolution of this marriage would be outweighed by the possible benefits which might accrue from the fact that this testimony might aid in the conviction of a criminal.

The question of which rule or rules of evidence *qua* rule or rules is justifiable would be answered by appeal to quite different considerations. Rather than delving into the strength of the bond between this particular husband and wife and passing upon the value of this marriage, the judge might begin by asking whether the presence of this rule had in fact tended to preserve familial peace and marital unity. He might look, for example, as Justice Stewart proposed in the *Hawkins* case, to the experiences of those jurisdictions which had employed a different husband-wife privilege. He might ask if allowing such testimony had tended to increase divorces and intrafamily conflict.[10] The judge might also refer, as did Justice Black in the *Hawkins* case, to evidence that tended to show that the prevention of irrevocable breaches between husband and wife is an important factor in the prevention of divorce. "The widespread success," Justice Black observed, "achieved by courts throughout the country in conciliating family differences is a real indication that some apparently broken homes can be saved provided no unforgivable act is done by either party. Adverse testimony given in criminal proceedings would, we think, be likely to destroy almost any marriage."[11]

The above two sketches help to indicate two important differences inherent in the kinds of evidence relevant in each of the two procedures. In the first place, evidence that would have been relevant to equitable justification of the *Hawkins* case is difficult to acquire. The judge, for example, could have formed an *intelligent* opinion about the strength of the *particular* marital bonds, if at all, only after he had been furnished with a comprehensive psychological study of the personalities of Hawkins and his wife. Also, a thorough social case-worker's study of the Hawkins marriage would seem to have been another prerequisite.[12] For how else could the judge have intelligently predicted the effect on the marriage of permitting the wife to testify *in this particular case*? It cannot be said that such evidence as this is never available, but certainly it rarely is. To require that this kind of evidence be presented in every case would surely serve to render the administration of justice more tedious; to permit decisions to be justified on equitable grounds without this kind of evidence would surely preclude the possibility of defensible decisions.

The contrary seems to be true of those questions which a judge would ask under a two-level theory. For here, that which is ultimately to be established, i.e., the desirability of the rule, is more susceptible to the ordinary methods of empirical investigation. The following experimental model would indicate the kind of evidence that should be sought. Suppose there are two jurisdictions, in one of which the *Hawkins rule* is adhered to, in the other of which spouses are permitted to testify against one another. And, suppose that the two jurisdictions are reasonably comparable except for this fact that two different rules of testimony are employed. Suppose further that there is one divorce per one hundred marriages in the jurisdiction in which the *Hawkins rule* is consistently applied, but that there are ten divorces per one hundred marriages in the other jurisdiction. Upon the presentation of evidence such as this it would surely be proper to infer that as a matter of fact the employment of a general husband-wife privilege does play a significant role in the preservation of marriages. Granted, data which show such a striking disparateness of effect cannot usually be found. But the important thing is that this is the kind of evidence that social scientists try to gather; it is the kind of evidence that can be fruitfully sought. Because the two-level procedure requires the court to formulate a rule of law that ought to be applied to all cases of a certain kind, it requires the court, of necessity, to formulate a hypothesis or set of hypotheses with respect to the consequences to society of this rule. And this hypothesis or set of hypotheses is amenable, at least in theory, to the usual kinds of objective examination and verification.

In this same connection, it is worth noting that such investigation and evaluation would not have to be undertaken each time a case involving the rule arose. The point here is wholly analogous to one made earlier. Under the two-level procedure of justification it is highly unlikely that new evidence sufficient to require a re-evaluation of the rule will be presented very often. Having found, for example, that the consistent application of the *Hawkins rule* resulted in fewer divorces than the application of an alternative rule, a court would not have to make a comparable study of the effects of these two rules every time a relevant case arose. Under the two-level procedure it would, of course, always be proper to introduce new evidence leading to a contrary inference, but this kind of evidence does not usually alter very rapidly. Moreover, it would always be permissible to show that there were heretofore unexamined factors which had been neglected and which ought to be taken expressly into account. But here again, the issue being raised would be circumscribed with considerable precision, and would for that reason be capable of being subjected to the same kind of systematic investigation.

These observations raise an objection to the two-level procedure that must be recognized. It relates to the burden that is placed upon the court by virtue of the fact that the court must justify its decisions in accordance with the most desirable legal rule. The objection is simply that the judiciary, under the two-level procedure, is forced to assume a role that is ordinarily thought to be that of the legislature. Since the two-level procedure expressly permits, and in fact demands, that courts "enact" legal rules, it would seem that the courts ought to engage in the same kinds of activities that a legislature should perform prior to enacting a workable and just statute. As has just been observed, evidence which purports to show the effect of a given rule or set of rules is often essential to the formulation and application by the court of a justifiable legal rule. Yet it is also plain that this is not the type of inquiry which is characteristic of the judicial enterprise. This is not the kind of evidence which is generally submitted to, or heard by, the courts.

It must be confessed that this is a problem for which there appears to be no easy answer. In part, the difficulties can be bypassed by observing that many of the issues with which the judiciary is concerned do not, even under the two-level procedure, necessitate this kind of investigation or analysis. But in part the issue must be confronted directly. Consideration of the alternatives is not especially helpful. If courts were to operate under a precedential decision procedure, it might be thought that the problem would not arise, for the courts would never have to decide whether an existing rule was a good rule. But even under a precedential procedure, a court, when faced with a case of "first impression," would have to formulate that rule which was destined to become the precedent. Moreover, since the doctrine of precedent requires that legal rules, once laid down, be applied in all subsequent cases, it seems to be even more important here than in other decision procedures that the court consider all evidence relevant to the question of what would be the best rule for this kind of case. Once the notion that legal rules are discovered rather than made by the courts is given up, it is difficult to escape the conclusion that these rules ought to be formulated intelligently. And if there is empirical evidence that tends to show which rules would be more desirable, it seems strange to suggest that this evidence ought to be systematically neglected.

Under the equitable decision procedure somewhat comparable inquiries would be demanded. For as was noted above, a defensible equitable decision could be rendered, if at all, only if the judge were supplied with evidence relating to such things as the personalities and capacities of the litigants. It can, however, be said in support of an equitable procedure that it would probably require the court to make the fewest kinds of "legislative" judgments. But this hardly constitutes a sufficient justification for its acceptance.

The dangers inherent in not permitting essentially "legislative" investigations become even more apparent when it is realized that even the weaker requirement, that courts give general reasons for their decisions, implies that at least some of these reasons cannot be evaluated in the absence of empirical evidence. For, to the extent to which the persuasiveness of the reasons depends upon the truth or falsity of descriptive propositions, precisely to that extent will the appropriateness of the reasons be unascertainable in the absence of supporting empirical evidence. Thus, although the workability of the two-level procedure does depend in part upon the presence of activities not customarily associated with the adjudication of cases, this appears to suggest that if courts are to adjudicate controversies in a reasoned and defensible manner, they must undertake these inquiries provided the situation so demands. To those who may find something "anti-legal" in any judicial recourse to "facts," empirical evidence, or scientific hypotheses, it can only be replied that the alternative is not "legality." It is, instead, unexamined and uncritical judicial enterprise.

The desirability of a two-level procedure of justification does not rest solely upon the character of the relevant inquiries and the accessibility of the relevant data. For the two-level procedure may tend to restrict the kinds of evaluations the judge is required to make. The issue here is as important as it is difficult to state clearly.

It is evident that if courts are to be permitted to alter existing legal rules or to introduce new ones (as is surely the case under the two-level procedure), this procedure cannot assure litigants that the decision in their case will not be influenced by "improper" considerations. The two-level procedure can guarantee neither the impartiality nor the omniscience of the person or persons entrusted with the obligations of evaluating legal rules and applying them correctly. A judge might miscalculate the consequences of a rule. He might, for reasons of bias or prejudice, introduce a rule that was not justifiable on any reasonable grounds. Or he might be confronted with a case for which no obviously desirable rule seems capable of formulation. The two-level procedure of justification cannot prevent the possibility of such occurrences; but it can tend to mitigate the effects of bias, mistake, and ignorance in a way in which the equitable procedure of justification might not.

It goes without saying that within either procedure of justification judges are required to make evaluations. But the proposition that courts must make normative judgments does not imply that they ought to be encouraged to make evaluations of all kinds. And it is, I submit, more desirable to urge a judge to make the kinds of evaluations required by the two-level procedure than it is to encourage him to make those demanded by a procedure of equitable adjudication. For as has already been indicated, it is one thing to permit the judge to decide whether the preservation of familial peace is desirable and whether a particular rule of evidence is conducive to that end. It is quite another thing to demand of the judge that he determine whether a *particular family* is worth preserving, or the degree to which a *particular litigant* will be made unhappy by a decision.[18]

In part, the analysis can be placed upon a historical basis. Within certain limits, experience has revealed the dangers inherent in an institution that permits judgments concerning which of two individuals, *as individuals,* can make better use of his assets, his talents, or his life. Perhaps the reason why so many societies insist, for instance, that the legislature enact rules which affect a class rather than an individual rests upon the distrust of evaluations of this particularity. Perhaps, too, when people have praised the desirability of "equality before the law," they have implicitly been referring not to the thesis that all people ought to be treated in the same fashion, but rather to the claim that all members of a specified class ought to be accorded like recognition.

In a related respect, the distinction between these two kinds of evaluations is analogous to the differences, discussed earlier, between an intuitive and a reasoned justification. If it is agreed that it is in general desirable for judges to specify as fully as possible the grounds upon which their decisions rest, then there is a sense in which the two-level procedure better succeeds in accomplishing this end. This is not to suggest that a judge who employed an equitable decision procedure would be less articulate in his written opinions. Nor is it to suggest that the judge could not state clearly, on equitable grounds, the reasons why he decided the case as he did. But it is to suggest at least the possibility that the two-level procedure imposes a greater burden upon the judge to make his reasons apparent. For to insist that a decision be justified by reference to some relevant, stated legal rule is to demand that the judge make explicit all the premises of his argument. To require the judge to reveal publicly which rule of law he deems most desirable, what it is that makes the rule justifiable, and how the decision in the case is thought to follow from these propositions is, perhaps, to demand something significant.

As we have noted several times, a requirement of this kind cannot ensure that judges will always select and employ correctly the most desirable rules of law. But it does help to ensure that the reasons the judge believes justify his decision will be expressly announced and will thereby be capable of independent scrutiny and disinterested criticism. If a judge is biased, or prejudiced, or simply incompetent, and sufficiently disingenuous, he can, no doubt, put his decisions into "respectable" two-level form. But still, to require even this judge to enunciate the rule that governs the decision, and the reasons that justify the rule, is to require him to indicate the justifications for the classification made and juridical consequences attached to that particular class of persons or actions. And if a judge is conscientious, the two-level procedure also serves as the means by which he can determine for himself whether the reasons he has given for the decision are in fact the kinds of reasons which can be accepted as good reasons.[14] By forcing the judge to ask how this *kind* of case ought to be treated by the legal system, the two-level procedure requires the judge to examine—in a way in which the equitable procedure cannot— the precise reasons for treating all cases of this kind in a certain fashion.

SOME OBJECTIONS TO THE TWO-LEVEL PROCEDURE

In the course of comparing the two-level and equitable procedures, certain possible objections to the two-level procedure were introduced and discussed; others were mentioned or deliberately overlooked at the time, and must now be confronted directly.

The first objection relates to the question of whether the requirement of *two* levels of justification is anything more than a rather artificial, highly formalistic formulation of a simpler, *one*-level procedure. In particular, in the light of what was said in Chapter 6 concerning the similarities between a careful restricted utilitarianism and a careful extreme utilitarianism, it might be argued that all that has been said so far could be stated far more concisely in terms of a procedure of justification which would require a court to consider in each case the long-term consequences of deciding that case in a certain fashion. In other words, it could be argued that the substantive equivalent of the two-level procedure would be a procedure whose rule of decision prescribed that a decision was justifiable if and only if all of the significant consequences of that decision were more desirable than those of any other. It could be argued, too, that the only function served by forcing the courts to talk in terms of two levels of justification is one of inducing the courts to accept familiar rules of law as desirable and of inviting judges to refuse to make exceptions—new rules—in those cases in which they ought to do so. And to make the case still more convincing, it could be noted that in every instance in which the two-level procedure seems to make a difference, i.e., in those cases in which the rule appears to work badly in a given case, there is strong prima facie evidence that another rule or set of rules, making an exception for this kind of litigant, or this kind of situation, ought to have been formulated in order to prevent the particular injustice. In short, there is nothing gained by employing a two-level procedure which could not be gained by utilizing an analogue of a careful extreme utilitarianism. And there is, in addition, much that might be gained were the latter to be adopted.

It must be conceded, for the reasons already stated in Chapter 6, that there are not any significant theoretical distinctions between a careful "extreme," or one-level, procedure of justification and a careful two-level procedure. But there do seem to be certain practical arguments which support the notion that the requirement of two levels of justification is not insignificant.

In the first place, it would clearly be a mistake to suppose that the fact of apparent or real injustices in a particular case necessarily implies that some better rule could have been formulated or that some more desirable decision could have been rendered. If the argument is that the two-level procedure is superfluous simply because every particular injustice will result in a new exception, the example of the poor widow and the rich mortgagee is an effective refutation. Even if some special rule for impoverished widows and wealthy mortgagees should be justifiable under the two-level procedure, such a rule would still probably insist that some mortgages be enforcible against some needy widows. Some widows might still be evicted simply because any "less severe" rule might have the effect of denying all widows the opportunity to borrow money.

All this being said, however, it nevertheless does seem to be true that there is a certain formalism about the two-level procedure. For once it is conceded, as I think it must be, that rules ought to be revised whenever a new, more justifiable rule can be shown to be capable of formulation and application, the stipulation that cases be decided by an appeal to rules appears to be less important. It is easy to see how the provision that cases be justified in accordance with a legal rule would be truly substantive were a precedential decision procedure to be employed. For here the character of the legal rule determines the justifiable decision. But if the relevant legal rule can be readily and indeterminately altered to "fit" each fact situation, the provision that cases be justified in accordance with legal rules is ostensibly formalistic precisely because the "relevant" legal rule is not itself necessarily determined prior to the time of litigation.

Even this formulation of the objection to the two-level procedure is not wholly fair. For as we have seen, the two-level procedure expressly insists that the *introduction* of the new, more desirable rule must be shown to be justifiable. It is not sufficient that an exception ought to be made to the existing rule; it must also be the case that the new rule, when introduced in place of the old one, would be more desirable. In addition to this argument and the others which were presented above in support of the two-level procedure, there is an argument of a rather different sort—although clearly only a practical one—which goes to the question of the kinds of exceptions which ought, in general, to be regarded as justifiable or unjustifiable. There are, in other words, additional reasons which have not yet been delineated, which tend to show that certain kinds of exceptions ought not to be made and that rules ought not to be altered despite the apparent hardship of applying them in a particular case. What must now be considered, therefore, in an admittedly imprecise and general fashion, are the reasons, relating to long-term consequences of a rather curious sort, for not making some kinds of exceptions to legal rules.

These arguments can best be introduced by means of an extreme example, one that illustrates many of the points made earlier in connection with the desirability of the two-level procedure, and that also indicates the form these additional arguments might take.

An important question arises concerning the degree to which blood-test evidence ought to be deemed conclusive in paternity cases. A child's blood type is inherited from its parents in accordance with relatively simple genetic laws. It is possible, if the blood types of a child and its mother are known, to exclude as possible fathers of that child all males having certain blood types. If these genetic laws of inheritance were altogether free from exceptions, there would be no problem about whether to regard the blood test of a putative father as capable of showing conclusively that he was not the father of the child. But unfortunately, inheritance of blood type does not always occur in accordance with these laws. In particular, although it is an extremely rare occurrence, mutation can occur in the child so that the child can be born with a blood type which is "incompatible" with the blood types of the parents. Thus, there is at least the possibility that a person accused of having fathered a child might be exonerated, if this test were to be regarded as conclusive, even though he was in fact the father.

It has been shown that the lowest possible per cent of probability of the test's being correct in any paternity case is 99 per cent. Under the most unfavorable circumstances a conclusion of nonpaternity based solely upon the test will be correct in 99 out of every 100 paternity cases.

Given these data, the problem raised is one of deciding the degree to which the blood test evidence is to be regarded as legally conclusive. If the test is genetically less than certain, it seems to follow that the legal conclusiveness of the test ought to reflect this uncertainty. For if the test is treated as legally conclusive, one child out of every one hundred may go fatherless simply because the real father denied paternity and the test "made a mistake."

In a thoughtful article dealing with the problems posed by this real possibility of error, Alf Ross presents the case for giving the test conclusive legal effect. And although the argument is clearly phrased in terms of long-term consequences, it is also, I think, an implicit argument for something like a two-level consideration of these long-term consequences.

If the ultimate end of the rules of evidence is that as many cases as possible be decided correctly, on the basis of assumed facts which are as near the truth as possible, the conclusion will certainly be that in all types of cases in which paternity is an issue blood-test exclusions must be recognized as unconditional and absolute proof. This rule requires that the judge refrain from any attempt to individualize the estimation of the evidence by taking into consideration contrary evidence offered by the mother to show that there are no other sources of paternity possible. If the legal certainty of the decision can be put at 99 per cent, and 20 cases arise each year, the judge, if the blood-test evidence is admitted as absolute, will give a right decision in 99 cases out of 100. The aim of an individualizing estimation of the evidence would be to make it possible to find precisely the one case which (every fifth year) can occur, in which, despite the blood-test exclusion, the mother is right and the man, in spite of everything, is indeed the father of her child. However, since the 100 cases do not come up for decision all together, but successively over 5 years and before different judges, there is no possibility of making a comparison and selecting the most reliable case. The result of an individualizing estimation of the evidence would inevitably be that the blood test would be set aside in more than 1 out of the 100 cases, which means that the average correctness of the legal decision would decrease. For example, if the blood test were set aside in 10 out of the 100 cases, 9 of the decisions would be wrong, and only 91, not 99, of the 100 cases would be decided correctly.

It is understandable that the judge, concerned intensively with the individual case and guided solely by the desire to give as just a decision as possible in that particular case, may be tempted to take into consideration such evidence as the "virtuous wife" may bring in the defense of her marriage, her child, and her honor, or such as the unmarried mother may bring to win support for her child. But in the interest of the presumed ultimate aim and purpose of evidentiary rules it must nevertheless be insisted that the individualizing estimation be rejected. There is no denying that individualizing would result in a considerable number of incorrect decisions, so that, for fear of committing an injustice against one innocent mother, injustices would be done to a number of alleged fathers.[15]

There are obvious similarities between this argument for giving the blood test conclusive effect and the argument presented earlier for not deciding mortgage cases on an equitable basis. But the blood-test example makes an even stronger point. In essence Ross's argument is simply that if the courts do not give the test conclusive effect, they will make more mistakes than they would if they always treated it as conclusive. Thus, even though the consistent application of this rule will lead to some results that are "bad," the rule ought to be employed in all cases simply because, given the present state of human knowledge, it will lead to fewer bad results than any alternative procedure. The interesting point is that the fact that injustice will result in some cases does not seem to give any support to the proposition that some new, more complicated rule of law could at present be devised in order to eliminate these injustices. The rule of legal conclusiveness of a blood test is the most justifiable rule even though it does not work in a wholly satisfactory way in all cases.

In the discussion earlier of widows and wealthy mortgagees, it was suggested that the two-level procedure left open the question of whether some new rule, taking special account of needy widows, would not be more desirable than the rule which made no such exception. The blood-test example does not show that such a rule necessarily ought not to be devised. But it does call attention to two other considerations that a judge ought always to consider before he introduces an exception of this kind.

The first consideration relates to the introduction of rules which have relatively little *generality*. Just as the judge in a paternity case cannot "pick out" the one case out of every 100 in which a mutation occurs, so too, it might be argued, the judge in a mortgage case cannot very successfully "pick out" those "exceptional" cases in which a rule different from the ordinary rule of mortgage transactions ought to be applied. If there is some rule of mortgage law which is in general clearly desirable, it could be maintained that the judge would render fewer bad decisions if he always applied that rule than he would were he to attempt to isolate just those cases in which the long-term consequences of invoking the rule would be undesirable. For it is one thing to be able to tell whether a case involving the enforcement of a mortgage is present, and a different thing, perhaps, to be able to pick out just that case or class of cases in which a widow ought to be given special treatment. This kind of argument can never be a wholly persuasive justification for refusing, a priori, to make an exception to a rule. But it does point out that one long-term consequence of employing rules that have relatively little generality is that mistakes of this kind may become more prevalent. This is, at least, another kind

of long-term consequence which ought to find explicit consideration in the justification of any new, less general rule.

The same point can be made in relation to the problems posed
by the *Hawkins* case. For there, too, the question of whether some
less encompassing formulation of the husband-wife privilege would
be more desirable than the one accepted by the Supreme Court
was expressly reserved for further consideration. And, indeed,
there is at least one recognized authority in the field of evidence,
Charles McCormick, who has suggested that the scope of the
privilege ought to be contracted. He argues that the

solution is to recognize, by statute, rule of court or decision, that the
privilege is not an absolute but a qualified one, which must yield if the
trial judge finds that the evidence of the communication is required in
the due administration of justice. The judge could then protect the
marital confidence when it should be protected, namely, when the material fact sought to be established by the communication is not sub-
stantially controverted and may be proven with reasonable convenience
by other evidence.[16]

In the light of what has been said throughout this chapter, it
should be evident that such a solution is compatible with the dictates of the two-level procedure. For what is proposed is a rule
that ought to be applied in all cases on the grounds, arguably,
that it is the most desirable rule of the husband-wife privilege.
However, in view of what has just been asserted concerning the
possible deleterious consequences of making rules which contain
too many exceptions, the grounds upon which McCormick's solution could be criticized are also apparent. That is to say, ·if it is
conceded that the husband-wife privilege is desirable (at least
in the absence of other circumstances), then the question which
must be asked is whether the presence of these other circumstances
that make it undesirable can be readily and correctly ascertained.
At a minimum, McCormick's solution can be shown to be more
desirable than the unqualified privilege accepted in the *Hawkins*
case only if it can be shown that the mistakes which the judge
would make in deciding when the privilege ought not to be allowed would be fewer and less harmful than the "mistakes" that
would occur were the privilege always permitted to prevail. As-

suming McCormick's initial premise, viz., that the privilege should not be allowed when the material facts cannot be proved with reasonable convenience by other evidence, it must still be demonstrated that the presence of this condition can be ascertained correctly in a sufficiently large number of cases in such a way as to overbalance the possible danger of denying the privilege in cases in which it ought to have been allowed.

Again, it perhaps deserves reiteration that this argument in no way implies that exceptions in the form of new rules ought not to be made, or that rules permitting the judge to exercise his "discretion" are incompatible with the two-level procedure. This argument only suggests that in addition to the reasons already given for the desirability of the two-level procedure, there may be an additional justification for not making exceptions of this order to legal rules. And requiring the justification of decisions to be phrased in terms of the relevant legal rules does have the practical effect of bringing these additional considerations more directly into view.

A second argument, related to the one outlined above, speaks to the question of the kinds of exceptions which ought to be made to legal rules. As we have seen, rules that contain too many exceptions can be criticized on the grounds that the probability of correct application is thereby diminished. Rules that embody exceptions of a different sort can also be criticized on the grounds that they make the "wrong" kinds of exceptions. Here the point is analogous to one made earlier in connection with the nature of the evidence which would be necessarily relevant to an equitable adjudication of cases. Because the equitable rule of decision prescribes that a decision is justifiable if and only if it produces a maximum of satisfaction and a minimum of dissatisfaction between the litigants, it was difficult to see how such things as the wealth, ages, sensibilities, capacities, and potentialities of the parties either could or should be deemed irrelevant to the rendering of a justifiable decision. And yet it was precisely factors of this nature with which it was thought the legal system ought to be unconcerned.[17] In view of the arguments just considered, it should be evident that there are similar justifications, founded upon a consideration of long-term consequences, for regarding certain kinds of characteristics as legally irrelevant. In essence, the argument is simply that if courts systematically refuse to attempt to evaluate certain kinds of individual characteristics, they will, in the long run, render more desirable decisions than they would were they to try to take them into account. Perhaps there are cases in which the wealth of the parties ought to be a relevant consideration. But it is so likely that the wealth of the respective parties will become a determining criterion in cases in which it should not even be considered that an argument surely exists for insisting that it should never be permitted to be relevant.

Now, what does all of this have to do with the practical desirability of the requirement of two levels of justification? The answer is simply this. By insisting that judges talk in terms of two levels of justification, by insisting that courts formulate and apply the most desirable rule of law, the two-level procedure requires the justification of these exceptions to be made explicit. Since the court is forced by the two-level procedure to articulate the applicable rule of law, the court is thereby required to show that the members of the class controlled by that rule ought to be treated in a certain fashion *because* they all possess that particular class characteristic.

It would be nice if one could say that all of the foregoing discussion is irrelevant because it is clear that courts ought to take account only of those considerations which are "legally relevant." But unfortunately, it does not seem to be possible to decide, a priori, that a certain characteristic is or is not legally relevant. The fact that children were for a long time regarded as no different from any other trespassers upon land does not necessarily imply that a special rule concerning child trespassers is less desirable than the more inclusive rule.[18] The fact that the husband-wife privilege is generally desirable does not necessarily imply that an exception ought not to be made for prostitute-procurer marriages. And since the categories of what should be legally relevant or irrelevant are neither static nor certain, the kinds of classifications that should be made by legal rules cannot be delimited once and for all. Thus, the best that can be done is to point out that there are considerations which should be weighed very carefully before rules which make certain kinds of distinctions ought to be regarded as good reasons for deciding a case. The two-level procedure alone has the virtue of requiring all such distinctions to be made explicit.

It should be evident that the preceding discussion of the two-level procedure—and in particular, the immediately preceding consideration of some possible objections to it—is also an answer to the question of whether moral rules ought to have a role in the process of adjudication. For if the suggestion that moral rules ought to play a significant role means that there are some moral rules which are more desirable than existing legal rules, then the two-level procedure explicitly permits such rules to be introduced. Since the class of legal rules cannot, under the two-level procedure, be delineated or circumscribed a priori, there does not appear to be any reason why those rules which are expressly moral rules, and which would also be the most desirable rules by which to adjudicate cases of a certain kind, could not be introduced into the legal system as the rules by which decisions in certain kinds of cases ought to be justified. If, for example, someone should argue convincingly that the moral rule which obliges a person to go to the aid of someone in obvious peril is more desirable as a potential legal rule than the present legal rule which imposes no such duty upon strangers, there do not seem to be any special reasons why this moral rule should not be introduced. The point is simply that the fact that a rule is a moral rule does not prevent it from also being made into a legal rule—provided, of course, it meets the requirements of justifiability imposed upon all rules by the two-level procedure. As long as the moral rule can be shown to be potentially the best legal rule for this kind of case, as long as justification in accordance with that moral rule can be shown to have more desirable consequences than justification in accordance with any other rule, the two-level procedure stipulates that that rule alone is what ought to count as a good reason for deciding cases of this kind in the fashion prescribed by that moral rule.

It must be recognized, finally, that the suggestion that cases be adjudicated in accordance with some moral rule or principle might mean something else. It might be a rejection of the desirability of utilitarian justification in general rather than an acceptance of the desirability of justification by means of those moral rules which are themselves justifiable on utilitarian grounds. As such, evaluation of this suggestion lies outside the boundaries of this inquiry. For at the outset it was assumed that the legal system ought to perform an essentially utilitarian function. It is significant to observe, however, that a suggestion of this kind need not be regarded as necessarily incompatible with the arguments heretofore advanced for the desirability of the two-level procedure of justification. Nor does such a view inevitably render the preceding arguments irrelevant. For if it should be maintained that the legal system ought to fulfill a function different from a utilitarian one, it would still be relevant to ask whether a procedure which used the formulation of that function as the criterion *by which to evaluate particular decisions* would be more desirable than one which invoked this criterion as the *justification for particular legal rules*. To the extent to which the arguments in this chapter were successful in showing the results of taking different kinds of consequences into account, and to the extent to which they were persuasive in demonstrating the *way* in which these considerations ought to be taken into account, they appear to be at least partially independent of the acceptance of a utilitarian function for the legal system. Given any seriously defensible role which the legal system ought to perform, it would still be meaningful to ask whether adoption of a two-level procedure of justification would not be the best means by which to achieve that goal. And if this question would still be a meaningful one, then the arguments for the two-level procedure would not, either immediately or inevitably, lose their persuasiveness upon the introduction of an avowedly nonutilitarian function.

Thus, although the introduction of a moral rule of this order might make it necessary to revise some of the proposals that were advanced and the conclusions drawn from them, it is not clear that a radical alteration of the basic theses of this chapter would be demanded. And unless the moral principle to be adopted would regard as clearly undesirable many of the kinds of consequences of which the principle of utility approves, it seems quite plausible to suppose that the arguments for the two-level procedure would continue to be appropriate even in this different moral context.

Irrespective of the extent to which a nonutilitarian legal system would find a two-level procedure to be desirable, it should be re-asserted that, even within an essentially utilitarian legal system, the two-level procedure of justification is not an all-inclusive solution to the problem of how cases ought to be decided. It is not a panacea which will dispel once and for all the pangs of uncertainty and doubt which necessarily afflict those who are engaged in the judicial enterprise. And its articulation is not even, perhaps, suggestive of a striking innovation in the character of judicial conduct. It is, instead, an attempt to bring into some kind of systematic program the more desirable features of alternative modes of decision. The two-level procedure is like the precedential decision procedure in its insistence that individual decisions be justifiable by appeal to relevant legal rules. It is unlike the precedential decision procedure in its insistence that the presence of an existing rule is not the sufficient justification for a decision. The two-level procedure is like the equitable decision procedure in its requirement that considerations of justice or utility be relevant to the justification of decisions. It is unlike the equitable decision procedure in its requirement that considerations of justice or utility be relevant to the justification of rules rather than particular decisions. Indeed, the two-level procedure may be very much like the procedure of justification most often described as that which the courts have in fact usually employed. For it may be indistinguishable from that procedure in which an existing legal rule is followed unless there is a "sufficient reason" for departing from that rule. If the two-level procedure herein described and examined is different from that procedure, it is so largely by virtue of the fact that a more meaningful and substantial content has been given to the notion of "sufficient reason."

8

Conclusion

In a real sense this inquiry has been an attempt to answer the question of whether reason or logic ought to have a significant function in the processes of judicial decision making. To this end we have examined various claims concerning the use of logic and reason in the law, and have delineated and evaluated three general procedures of legal justification. And we have concluded that the two-level procedure, although in itself not wholly free from defects, best embodies the characteristics that any procedure of legal justification ought to possess. To urge that courts ought to employ a two-level procedure of justification is to assert that a rational decision process is both possible and desirable.

It perhaps bears repeating that there are at least two respects in which the properties of a "rational" decision procedure are correctly attributable to the two-level procedure of justification. First, before any particular decision is deemed to have been truly justified, it must be shown to be formally deducible from some legal rule. Here, the ordinary canons of logic would be employed to determine whether the conclusion reached indeed follows from the premises selected. To insist that legal justification be logical in this sense is to impose no greater and no lesser requirement here than in most other types of argumentation and justification. But the familiarity of the requirement does not excuse its neglect. Although questions relating to the formal validity of an argument may be only preliminary to an examination of the material desirability of the premises assumed, they are among the most important of preliminary questions. To require that judicial decisions be deducible from legal rules is to do more than insist that an argument not be formally fallacious. For it is to ensure as well that further criticism and evaluation of the premises of that argument will be possible; it is to require that the grounds of decision be made articulate so that their content will be understandable and their correctness verifiable. The demand that the procedure of justification be logical in this sense does not assure that just decisions will be forthcoming; but it does hold out the promise that the reasons which purport to justify decisions can be subjected to independent scrutiny and objective verification.

Second, before any particular decision is deemed to have been truly justified, the rule upon which its justification depends must be shown to be itself desirable, and its introduction into the legal system itself defensible. The two-level procedure expressly provides that only those premises, those legal rules, whose implementation has been ascertained to be conducive to the production of socially desirable consequences, can count as good reasons for individual judicial decisions. The techniques of empirical inquiry are as essential to the production of reasoned legal justifications as they are to the successful operation of any other social program that relies upon the truth or falsity of descriptive claims. The characteristics of intellectually persuasive argumentation are as necessary to the presentation of commendable legal justifications as they are to the defense of any other decision of normative significance.

A procedure of legal justification that unequivocally employed the two-level logic of justification would be, therefore, thoroughly rationalistic in both of these important respects.

In a real sense, too, this inquiry has been an endeavor to assess the relationship between the two-level procedure of justification and the suggestion that the legal decision process be pragmatic, sociological, realistic, or "free." Such a task is not easy. For as has been indicated throughout, the prevalence of the "call" for a jurisprudence of these kinds has not been matched by a corresponding elucidation of what such procedures would be like.

If the demand for a new approach to the problems of adjudication implies that rational judicial evaluation of the kind just discussed has no place within the processes of decision, then an advocacy of the two-level procedure of justification is inconsistent with the tenets of recent philosophical thought. If the request that courts decide cases realistically or "freely" implies that they cannot and should not seek out those rules, principles, or conceptions upon which their decisions ought to be founded, then acceptance of the two-level procedure clearly requires the rejection of a realistic or "free" decision process on both factual and normative grounds. If the assertion that "The life of the law has not been logic: it has been experience" means—as some seem to have supposed—that instinctive or intuitive or visceral reactions are to be deemed the trustworthy signal that a proper judicial decision has been reached, then it can only be reasserted that a justificatory procedure which adopts these criteria is indefensible. In this sense the foregoing inquiry has been openly antagonistic and deliberately reformative.

In another sense, however, the entire investigation—and in particular the espousal of the two-level procedure of justification—can be conceived to be explicative of recent philosophic thought. To insist, for example, that "the felt necessities of the time, the prevalent moral and political theories . . . [and] even the prejudices which judges share with their fellow-men, have had a good deal more to do than the syllogism in determining the rules by which the law should be governed"[1] might mean only that rules of law have often been selected on improper grounds, and that formal logic, among other things, is not a tool which enables the correctness or desirability of these rules to be assessed. With this the two-level procedure has no quarrel. Rather, it is an attempt to specify more precisely the grounds upon which any rules of law ought to be applied or overruled. If the deprecation of "mechanical" or "deductive" decision procedures is only an attack upon an unanalyzed and uncritical judicial acceptance of existing rules and principles, then the two-level procedure may be construed as a means by which a *critical* acceptance or rejection of existing rules becomes possible.

Nor is there any apparent incompatibility between the function that the two-level procedure of justification assigns to legal rules and the function suggested by exponents of pragmatic or experimental jurisprudence.

The legal rule enunciated in a decision becomes but a "working hypothesis" which will be demonstrated experimentally to be sound or unsound. The rule will be just or unjust as its consequences reveal. As law for Justice Holmes means prophecies of what the court will do; so just law for the pragmatist jurist means prophecies of what will produce the most satisfactory and most desired consequences, in the main and on the whole view.[2]

It should be evident that an adherence to the two-level procedure seems quite inevitably to require that legal rules be regarded as nothing more than "working hypotheses." Indeed, the arguments advanced in the preceding chapter were designed specifically to elucidate more carefully of what this "in-the-main-and-on-the-whole view" consists.

If, in similar fashion, a sociological decision process would be one in which the best evidence obtainable from all fields of empirical inquiry would be the basis upon which rules of law were to be formulated and evaluated, the two-level procedure is itself sociological in part. It expressly insists upon the relevance of just such evidence.

Thus, the conclusions reached in the course of this investigation are diametrically opposed to the first of these two interpretations of modern legal philosophy. Particularistic and nonrational justification has no place within the operation of the decision procedure here deemed most desirable. The conclusions of this inquiry are, however, just as certainly in conformity with the second interpretation; but that is only because both claim membership in a far older and more firmly established philosophical tradition—the tradition that proclaims the rewards of reasoned inquiry and the virtues of enlightened action.

Notes

᠎᠎

Full titles and publication data will be found in the Bibliography.

NOTES TO CHAPTER TWO

1. See, among others, Frank, *Law and the Modern Mind*; Pound, "Mechanical Jurisprudence"; Cohen, *Law and the Social Order*; and Bodenheimer, "Analytic Positivism, Legal Realism, and the Future of Legal Method."

2. Fuller, in his Introduction to Schoch, ed., *The Jurisprudence of Interests*, p. xix.

3. One of the relatively few unambiguous examples of adherence to the deductive theory is found in a remark that Fuller attributes to Langdell. Fuller reports that when Langdell was "confronted with an assertion that one of the results demanded by his system was 'contrary to substantial justice and the interests of the contracting parties,' Langdell replied blandly that considerations of this sort are 'irrelevant'" (*ibid.*).

Also, I do not mean to assert that comparable judicial pronouncements cannot be located. In the case of *Gluck v. Baltimore* (81 Md. 315, 32 A 515, 1895), for example, the court can be read as asserting that the "logical" application of an existing rule is more important than the consequences of the rule. There the court noted that: "Obviously a principle, if sound, ought to be applied wherever it logically leads, without reference to ulterior results. That it may in consequence operate in some instances with apparent or even real harshness and severity does not indicate that it is inherently erroneous. Its consequence in special cases can never impeach its accuracy" (p. 325).

As I have said, though, explicit assertions of this kind are far less prevalent than would be supposed.

4. *Lochner v. New York*, 198 U.S. 45, 76 (1905), Holmes, J. dissenting. Holmes, *The Common Law*, p. 1.

5. Stone, *The Province and Function of Law*, p. 170.

6. Holmes, "The Path of the Law," pp. 465–66.

7. Several proponents of the view that the deductive theory is inadequate have sought to give further explanations of why judges disguise

the way in which they reach their decisions. (One of the most notable and controversial explanations is to be found in Frank, pp. 13–20.) A point which Frank and others often fail to realize, however, is that such an explanation is quite irrelevant to the question of *whether* the process is in fact "deductive."

8. Stone, p. 170; Frank, pp. 9, 24.

9. *The Standard Oil Co. of New Jersey v. United States,* 221 U.S. 1 (1911); *United States v. The American Tobacco Co.,* 221 U.S. 106 (1911).

10. Frank, p. 24.

11. Stone, p. 181.

12. [1932] A.C. 562.

13. Stone, pp. 181–82. Italics mine. For other examples which are presented as illustrative of the nondeductive character of the legal decision process, see: Llewellyn, "The Rule of Law in Our Case-Law of Contracts"; Llewellyn, "The Status of the Rule of Judicial Precedent"; Levi, *An Introduction to Legal Reasoning*; and Radin, "Case Law and Stare Decisis."

14. Cf., for example, Radin, *Law as Logic and Experience,* p. 51; Oliphant, "A Return to Stare Decisis," pp. 72–73; and Frank, p. 268 n.: "in a profound sense *the unique circumstances of almost any case make it an 'unprovided case.'* "

15. Allen, *Law in the Making,* pp. 241–42.

16. Oliphant, p. 72.

17. See, in particular, Hutcheson, "The Judgment Intuitive: The Function of the 'Hunch' in Judicial Decisions" and "Lawyer's Law and the Little, Small Dice."

18. Oliphant, p. 159. Italics mine.

19. Frank, p. 106.

20. For examples of this position see Stoljar, "The Logical Status of a Legal Principle," and Williams, "Language and the Law."

21. Williams, Part V, §8. Williams's analysis of legal rules is ambiguous, however, since he never makes it clear whose desire is expressed by the legal rule. At times he seems to feel it is the judge's desire that is expressed (cf. p. 397). At other times he implies that it is the desire of the person or persons who made the rule which the judge simply applies (cf. p. 398). And at still other times he argues that a rule arouses desires or emotions in others (cf. *ibid.*).

22. I refer to statements of the following kind as possible candidates: "It is, however, extremely likely that if a technically precise system of logical rules were devised for proceeding from evidence to the facts sought to be proved, our sense of being surely in possession of these facts—always remembering that only a selection of the relevant facts is possible or attempted—will not have been greatly enhanced. *Our definitions and postulates will still be arbitrary even if handled with greater*

skill than we now handle them." Radin, *Law as Logic and Experience,* p. 58. Italics mine.

"*Under the guise of logic, then, we have methods purely arbitrary, everything depending on the choice of the major premise.* This is not objectionable as method; the abuse lies in applying logic in the proper sphere of the empirical." Oliphant and Hewett, in their Introduction to Rueff, *From the Physical to the Social Sciences,* p. xxi. Italics mine.

"There is no rule by which you can force a judge to follow an old rule or by which you can predict when he will verbalize his conclusion in the form of a new rule, or by which he can determine when to consider a case as an exception to an old rule, *or by which he can make up his mind whether to select one or another old rule to explain or guide his judgment.*" Frank, p. 128. Italics mine.

23. Mr. Justice Holmes's famous passage in *The Common Law* (p. 1) illustrates the kind of statement that lends itself to a variety of interpretations. The passage reads: "The life of the law has not been logic: it has been experience. The felt necessities of the time, the prevalent moral and political theories, intuitions of public policy, avowed or unconscious, even the prejudices which judges share with their fellow-men, have had a good deal more to do than the syllogism in determining the rules by which men should be governed."

Even if the passage is regarded as purely descriptive of the way in which cases have been decided, it is not easy to see why this particular conjunction should be established. If the syllogism has not had very much to do with determining the rules of law, why must the crucial factors have been such things as "felt necessities," "intuitions," and "prejudices"? Granted, Holmes might not be saying that these things have been determinative because the syllogism has not. He might only be saying that regardless of what might have been determinative, these things have in fact been influential. On the other hand, by announcing at the outset that the life of the law has been that of experience rather than logic, and by then giving an explication of what he conceives the characteristics of "experience" to be, Holmes seems to suggest that if the syllogism (logic) has not been operative, then such things as intuitions, felt necessities, and prejudices must have been present and determinative. Interpreted in this way, Holmes seems to have committed the irrationalist fallacy, particularly since he appears to have no difficulty in identifying moral and political theories with felt necessities, intuitions, and prejudices.

24. See Beard, *An Economic Interpretation of the Constitution.*

25. I know of only two legal philosophers who have attempted to make a comparable distinction. One is Hermann Kantorowicz, "Some Rationalism about Realism," 43 Yale Law Journal 1240 (1934): "The question chiefly interesting the judge is whether the decision he wants to give can be justified as a consequence of the particular statute, or at

least as being compatible with its consequences. . . . Genetic explanation and normative justification must be kept apart—this is one of the
most important lessons of modern epistemology" (*ibid.*, p. 1249). The
other is Max Radin, whose article entitled "The Method of Law," Washington University Law Quarterly 471 (1950), is a systematic analysis
of several different processes of judicial justification.

    26. Frank, pp. 100, 128.

    27. *Ibid.*, pp. 130, 131.

    28. Hart, "Positivism and the Separation of Law and Morals," pp.
607, 610. This article is one of the clearest and most important contributions to the field of legal philosophy that has been produced. One of
its many virtues is that it shows the speciousness of so many of the
attacks upon the so-called legal positivists. Hart's essay draws many of
the same distinctions that this chapter is attempting to make.

    29. Hart, for example, presents just such an argument (see p. 607).
Although not directly relevant to the subject of this inquiry, it should
be noted that Fuller attacks Hart on just this point in his article entitled
"Positivism and Fidelity to Law—A Reply to Professor Hart," pp. 661–
69. There Fuller suggests that Hart's view necessarily implies that legal
rules must be applied solely on the basis of the standard meanings of
the terms of the rule—provided the fact situation is a clear instance of
the standard meaning—without regard for the purpose of the legal rule.
If Fuller has correctly understood Hart, then his objection seems to have
considerable merit, at least in some contexts. But it is surely plausible
to read Hart as seeking to maintain a considerably weaker thesis—
namely, that it is only because there are "standard instances" of meaning that it is possible to ask in any meaningful fashion about the purpose
of a legal rule. Granted, Hart does not develop his remarks about the
"core of meaning" very fully. But it is at least possible, and I think
plausible, to read him as saying only that problems relating to the purpose of a legal rule may not arise very often when the case in question
is a "standard instance."

    30. Hart, p. 607. I do not mean to suggest that Hart here gives up
the possibility of justifying a "penumbral" classification. On the contrary, his point is rather that "if legal arguments and legal decisions of
penumbral questions are to be rational, their rationality must lie in
something other than a logical relation to premises. So if it is rational
or 'sound' to argue and to decide that for the purpose of this rule an
airplane is not a vehicle, this argument must be sound or rational without being logically conclusive" (p. 608). This is the same distinction
which I seek to make between the notion of "logical validity" and that
of a "good reason."

    31. Statements to this effect can be found in almost any standard
text on legal method. See, for example, Allen, pp. 223, 243.

    32. 9 Exch. 341, 156 Eng. Rep. 145 (Ex. 1854).

33. *Kerr Steamship Co. v. Radio Corporation of America*, 245 N.Y. 284 (1927); *Restatement of Contracts*, §330; McCormick, *Handbook on the Law of Damages*, §138.

34. McCormick, pp. 564–65.

35. Another example would be the so-called rule in *Shelley's Case*.

36. I do not want to become involved in the controversy over the correct or appropriate definition of "law," or the question of to whom laws are addressed. There are obviously alternative ways in which laws could be defined or described. It might be noted, however, that definitions of "law" phrased in terms of "what the courts will do" or "what the courts have done" will not prove very useful to a judge who is asking himself what law applies, or ought to apply, to a given case.

37. For example, the rule of contract law relating to the time at which the acceptance to a contract becomes operative might be put into the form: "If the acceptance of an offer to make a contract is mailed prior to the time the offer is revoked, then the acceptance is operative." Or it might be put into the form: "All acceptances of offers to make a contract that are mailed prior to the revocation of the offer are operative."

It should be noted that such formulations may be misleading if not read within the context of many other possibly relevant rules. That is, I am assuming that the only issue with which the court is concerned is whether an offer may be revoked once the acceptance has been mailed. Whether the "law of contracts," where stated wholly in terms of rules that provide the necessary and sufficient conditions for enforcible contracts, is a somewhat misleading way of viewing the import of the legal concept of contract, is a question which for my purposes can be neglected.

For an argument that such a formulation is possibly misleading, see H. L. A. Hart, "The Ascription of Responsibility and Rights."

38. Kelsen, for instance, in "The Pure Theory of Law," p. 478, suggests that "a parliamentary ruling, a judicial sentence, a legal process, a delict" are all called "law."

39. Pound, "The Theory of Judicial Decision." Pound here distinguishes among several different kinds of legal propositions, although not in the same way I have.

NOTES TO CHAPTER THREE

1. Salmond, "The Theory of Judicial Precedents."

2. *Ibid.*, p. 377.

3. This view is also discussed below, pp. 65–66.

4. Salmond, pp. 378–81.

5. *Sheddon v. Goodrich*, 8 Ves. 481, 497. 32 Eng. Rep. 441, 447 (Ch. 1803).

6. Salmond, pp. 383–84.

7. *Ibid.*, p. 385.

8. Black, *Handbook on the Law of Judicial Precedents*, pp. 2–3.

9. Allen, *Law in the Making*, pp. 273–74.

10. Cf. *ibid.*, p. 276.

11. Salmond, p. 381.

12. *Ibid.*

13. *United States v. South-Eastern Underwriters Association*, 322 U.S. 533, 594 (1944).

14. Salmond, p. 386.

15. As has been observed, most English authors would not give complete assent to this proposition. Both Salmond and Allen, for instance, insist that conditions of defeasance may be part of the doctrine. There are, nevertheless, some English commentators who appear to accept without qualification the premise that a precedent must always be followed. Cf. Holdsworth, "Case Law." There are, as well, several important English cases which enunciate such a doctrine quite explicitly as binding upon the House of Lords (see Chap. 4).

16. Radin, "Case Law and Stare Decisis," pp. 199 and following.

17. *Ibid.*, p. 212.

18. Von Moschzisker, "Stare Decisis in Courts of Last Resort," pp. 412, 414.

19. Cahn, *The Sense of Injustice*, p. 14.

Law," p. 363.

20. Ellenbogen, "The Doctrine of Stare Decisis and the Extent to Which It Should Be Applied," p. 504.

21. Radin, p. 200.

NOTES TO CHAPTER FOUR

1. 10 Clark and Fin. 534; 8 Eng. Rep. 844 (1844).

2. 9 H.L.C. 274; 11 Eng. Rep. 735 (1861).

3. *Ibid.*, pp. 334–39.

4. Wade, "The Concept of Legal Certainty," p. 185.

5. Patterson, *Jurisprudence*, p. 97.

6. Bodenheimer, "Law as Order and Justice," p. 199.

7. Goodhart, "Precedent in English and Continental Law."

8. *Ibid.*, p. 58.

9. Cf. Bodenheimer, "Law as Order and Justice," p. 196: "The yearning of human beings for order, regularity, and predictability in the operation of social and governmental processes is responsible for a characteristic concomitant of legal regulation which we shall designate the *normative* element in law."

10. The argument can also be put in terms of the effect upon those subject to the legal system. A legal system which lacked this character-

istic of stability entirely would, it is claimed, serve only to make people "as uncomfortable and helpless in the social order as they would be in a chaotic and unpredictable physical universe." Bodenheimer, *ibid.*, p. 199.

11. Wigmore, *Problems of Law*, p. 79, quoted in Goodhart, "Case Law in England and America," p. 185.

12. *Lee v. Jones*, 224 La. 231, 250–51 (1953). It is interesting to note that Louisiana is the only jurisdiction in the United States whose system of law is based upon the French Civil Code. Code systems are not usually thought to be committed to the doctrine of precedent (see, e.g., the quotation from Wigmore cited above).

13. *Kerr Steamship Co. v. Radio Corporation of America*, 245 N.Y. 284, 291 (1927). See also Cardozo, *The Paradoxes of Legal Science*, pp. 70–71.

14. Llewellyn, "Case Law," p. 249.

15. Cahn, *The Sense of Injustice*, p. 14.

16. Berlin, "Equality," esp. pp. 313–14.

17. *Ibid.*, p. 306.

18. *Ibid.*, pp. 302–3, 305. "To provide no reasons for breaking a rule is described as irrational; to give reasons for obeying rules—save in terms of other rules—is regarded as unnecessary" (pp. 306–7).

19. Cahn, *The Sense of Injustice*, p. 14.

20. Cardozo, *The Nature of the Judicial Process*, pp. 149–50. See also Llewellyn, *The Bramble Bush*, pp. 64–65.

21. Goodhart, "Precedent in English and Continental Law."

22. *Ibid.*, pp. 49–50.

23. Quoted in *ibid.*, pp. 54, 55.

24. *Ibid.*, p. 56.

25. *The London Street Tramways Company Ltd. v. The London County Council*, [1898] A.C. 375, 379–80. Italics mine.

A somewhat similar argument is perhaps to be found in Dias and Hughes, *Jurisprudence*, p. 53: "It is impossible to furnish a legal reason why precedents *ought* to be binding; the only answer that can be given is that the manner in which they are treated is an assumption on which the system now rests. We may trace historically *how* it evolved, but we shall not find an explanation in law or principle *why* it should be so."

NOTES TO CHAPTER FIVE

1. Kipling, "The Ameer's Homily," quoted in Pound, "Justice According to Law," p. 697 n.

2. *In re* Egan, 5 Blatchford 319, 321 (1866), quoted in *ibid.*, p. 697.

3. Cf., for instance, Pound's thesis that there are two fundamental elements present in all mature legal systems, namely, the "legal" and

the "discretionary." "Before the law we have justice without law; and after the law and during the evolution of law we still have it under the name of discretion, or natural justice, or equity and good conscience, as an anti-legal element." Pound, "The Decadence of Equity," p. 20.

4. *Cobb v. Whitney*, 124 Okla. 188, 192 (1926); *Kenyon v. Weissberg*, 240 F. 536, 537 (1917).

5. Pomeroy, *A Treatise on Equity Jurisprudence*, pp. 46–47; Phelps, *Elements of Juridical Equity*, §143; Frank, *Law and the Modern Mind*, p. 157; Stone, *The Province and Function of Law*, pp. 228–29.

6. Oliphant, "A Return to Stare Decisis," p. 159. Italics mine.

7. Hutcheson, "The Judgment Intuitive," p. 285. As is characteristic of one who adheres to an intuitive scheme of justification, Hutcheson resorts at times to rather mystical statements of approval. He announces, for example, that: "It is such judicial intuitions, and the opinions lighted and warmed by the feeling which produced them, that not only give justice in the cause, but like a great white way, make plain in the wilderness the way of the Lord for judicial feet to follow" (pp. 287–88).

8. Frank, p. 121. See also Gmelin, "Sociological Method," in *Science of Legal Method*, p. 100, where he seems to be proposing a similar view: "We need a vivid understanding of the facts, a sympathetic treatment of the human destinies that are passing before our eyes. We must strive to penetrate into the needs of the parties who come before the judge as patients come before the physician, so that we may not offer them the stone of bald reasoning but the bread of sympathetic relief."

9. Pound, "Mechanical Jurisprudence," p. 605.

10. Dewey, "Logical Method and Law," p. 24.

11. Pound, "The Theory of Judicial Decision," pp. 951–52.

12. Although giving a somewhat different justification for treating all contract and property cases in a manner different from tort and other analogous kinds of cases, Dickinson seems to adopt Pound's rationale at least in part. For he agrees with Pound that there is a field in which "every case involves a multitude of pertinent elements which vary in importance from case to case, [and therefore] it is practically impossible fairly to select any special factor or factors and apply them as criteria over the whole field. This is true of all ordinary matters of conduct not definitely directed, like business transactions, to the production of a legal result." Dickinson, *Administrative Justice and the Supremacy of Law*, pp. 145–46.

13. *Hynes v. New York Central RR. Co.*, 231 N.Y. 229, 231 (1921).

14. *Herter v. Mullen*, 159 N.Y. 28, 41–42 (1899).

15. Pound, "The Theory of Judicial Decision," p. 951.

16. Cf., for instance, Frank, pp. 118–19, and Patterson, *Jurisprudence*, p. 582. Cf. also Salmond, *Jurisprudence*, p. 83: "For the law

lays down general principles, taking of necessity no account of the special circumstances of individual cases in which such generality may work injustice. . . . In all such cases, in order to avoid injustice, it may be considered needful to go beyond the law, or even contrary to the law, and to administer justice in accordance with the dictates of natural reason."

For a judicial expression of the same view see *Berkel v. Berwind-White Coal Mining Co.,* 220 Pa. 65 (1908): "The whole system of equity jurisprudence is founded on the theory that the law, by reason of its universality, is unable to do justice between the parties, and equity, not being bound by common-law forms and pleadings, has more elasticity and can better reach this end" (p. 75).

Ehrlich seems to make a still stronger assertion along the same lines: "It is certain that one need not expect better or juster results from such technical decisions than from free ones. Generally speaking, it is undoubtedly much easier to decide a definite case correctly than to establish an abstract rule universally applicable for all imaginable cases; and surely it can hardly be maintained seriously that such a rule will invariably result in the fairest decision, even in those cases which nobody had thought of when the rule was made." (Ehrlich, "Judicial Freedom of Decision," in *Science of Legal Method,* p. 63.)

The dichotomy, as set up by Ehrlich, appears convincing. The difficult problem, however, concerns the ways, if any, in which knowing that a definite case has been decided correctly differs from formulating and applying a rule for that kind of case. If a case cannot be decided correctly without laying down a rule, then the argument advanced by Ehrlich seems less attractive. See Chaps. 6 and 7, in which this point is explored in detail.

17. Aristotle, *Nicomachean Ethics,* 1137b, 12–29.

18. *Ibid.,* 20.

19. Swiss Civil Code, Article I. See also Cardozo, *The Nature of the Judicial Process,* pp. 142–43.

20. Patterson, p. 582.

21. *Webb v. McGowin,* 27 Ala. App. 82 (1935).

NOTES TO CHAPTER SIX

1. Among the better-known writings on this subject are: Brown, "Utilitarianism and Moral Obligation"; McCloskey, "An Examination of Restricted Utilitarianism"; Melden, "Two Comments about Utilitarianism"; Rawls, "Two Concepts of Rules"; Nowell-Smith, *Ethics;* Smart, "Extreme and Restricted Utilitarianism"; and Toulmin, *The Place of Reason in Ethics.*

2. Cf., for example, Nowell-Smith, pp. 236–37; Brandt, *Ethical Theory*, p. 397; and Rawls, pp. 4–13.

3. This can be said without raising the question of whether utilitarianism is, in either form, a desirable moral philosophy.

4. Austin, *The Province of Jurisprudence Determined*, pp. 47–48. It is of some historical interest to observe that arguments for an essentially restricted utilitarian position can even be found in some of the earlier utilitarian philosophers. Hobbes, for instance, presents a decidedly restricted utilitarian justification for entering into civil society. And Hume does the same in his justification for the institution of property. See, for example, Hobbes, *Leviathan*, Chap. XV; Hume, *Treatise of Human Nature*, Bk. III, Part II, §3. And see also Urmson, "The Interpretation of the Philosophy of J. S. Mill."

5. Toulmin, p. 151.

6. Smart, p. 347.

7. *Ibid.*, pp. 348–49.

8. Toulmin, p. 146.

9. Nowell-Smith, p. 239.

10. Smart, p. 346.

11. Toulmin, p. 146.

12. Rawls, pp. 26–27.

13. Nowell-Smith, pp. 236–37.

14. Rawls, pp. 16, 24.

15. Cf. *supra*, pp. 110–11.

16. Restricted utilitarianism is sometimes formulated as requiring a "direct" appeal to the principle of utility whenever there is a conflict of relevant moral rules. Once this is permitted, however, all significant moral decisions almost surely become justifiable only on extreme utilitarian grounds. Restricted utilitarianism now provides a justificatory scheme only for those acts in which there is little or no doubt concerning what course of conduct is morally justifiable.

NOTES TO CHAPTER SEVEN

1. As a matter of fact, the history of Anglo-American mortgage law can probably be read to support the hypothesis that prospective mortgagees have been willing to lend money even though the courts give considerable protection to the necessitous mortgagor. The argument presented above is not to be construed, therefore, as claiming that mortgage transactions would disappear from society if mortgagees were granted anything less than an absolute remedy of strict foreclosure. It only suggests that mortgage transactions might become uncommon once the remedies afforded to mortgagees reached a certain degree of ineffectuality.

2. See *infra*, pp. 162–68.

3. *Webb v. McGowin,* 27 Ala. App. 82 (1935).
4. *Hawkins v. United States,* 358 U.S. 74 (1958).
5. *Ibid.,* p. 77.
6. *Supra,* pp. 60–62.
7. Changes of this kind do of course occur. The innovations in mortgage law which became necessary as a result of the depression of the 1930's provide one such example.
8. A proposal such as this is not original with the author. The best-known article advocating such a procedure is that by Kocourek and Koven, "Renovation of the Common Law Through Stare Decisis."
9. In opposition to a view such as the one just outlined, arguments of the following kind are not unusual: "It is the function of the courts to construe the written law and to apply the unwritten law, and while the unwritten law is sometimes referred to as 'judge-made law' it would be a serious mistake and lead to a perversion of our whole judicial system to avow that judges have the right to create law and to announce a rule of law which is to be followed in the future, but which is not to be applied to the past. Only the legislature has the right to do that." (Henry Ellenbogen, "The Doctrine of Stare Decisis and the Extent to Which It Should Be Applied," p. 514.)

The prevalence of the argument does not make it any easier to understand. If courts should be permitted to alter existing precedents and if it is conceded that these precedents were themselves created by other courts, there does not seem to be any reason why courts should not be able to take into account the manner in which the "new" precedent ought to be given legal effect. If there is a truly good example of "mechanical" jurisprudence, it is probably the doctrine that once a precedent is overruled or altered it never existed regardless of what potential litigants and attorneys may have thought and done to the contrary.

10. *Hawkins v. United States,* 358 U.S. 74, 82 n.4 (1958), concurring opinion.
11. *Ibid.,* pp. 77–78.
12. Interestingly enough, Radin, among others, makes an express plea for just such evidence:

"I have suggested that whenever a case involving the economic and social relations of two persons comes before the court for decision, the court should undertake a study of the personal and environmental histories of these persons which would somewhat resemble the study that Robert and Helen Lynd made of Middletown; and that in a criminal case it would be a criminological study as documented as a psychiatric case history which could be appended to a book comparable to Hooton's book on the American criminal or the Gluecks' study of delinquent children." Radin, *Law as Logic and Experience,* p. 51.

13. In a recent thoughtful article entitled "Toward Neutral Prin-

ciples of Constitutional Law," Professor Herbert Wechsler presents the outlines of a theory of adjudication which does seem to be rather analogous to the two-level procedure herein being developed and proposed. At the very least, several of his observations are peculiarly relevant to the arguments I have explored. In particular, in relation to the point now under discussion, Professor Wechsler says (admittedly in a different context): "The man who simply lets his judgment turn on the immediate result may not, however, realize that his position implies that the courts are free to function as a naked power organ, that it is an empty affirmation to regard them, as ambivalently as he often does, as courts of law. If he may know he disapproves of a decision when all he knows is that it has sustained a claim put forward by a labor union or a taxpayer, a Negro or a segregationist, a corporation or a Communist—he acquiesces in the proposition that a man of different sympathy but equal information may no less properly conclude that he approves" (p. 12).

This passage can be quoted with approval without endorsing Professor Wechsler's interpretation of certain recent Supreme Court cases in which, he suggests, this kind of judgment may have been made by the Court.

14. See *ibid.*, p. 19: "A principled decision, in the sense I have in mind, is one that rests on reasons with respect to all the issues in the case, reasons that in their generality and their neutrality transcend any immediate result that is involved."

15. Ross, "The Value of Blood Tests as Evidence in Paternity Cases," pp. 482–83.

16. McCormick, *Evidence*, p. 180.

17. See Wechsler, p. 12.

18. See the justification offered by Edmond Cahn, for instance, for making just such an exception in the "attractive nuisance" cases, i.e., those cases which involve children who have trespassed upon someone else's property (often a railroad's) in order to play with or upon some piece of machinery there, and who have been injured while so playing. Cahn suggests that children ought to be treated differently from ordinary trespassers because:

"When a child looks, he sees what he may never be able to see again because his sight is not yet obscured by associations of the past or restricted by motives pointing to the future. . . . He has the right to be young, that is, to live in lyric immediacy, intensity, and irresponsibility, to observe—not in order to serve some imperious further purpose but simply and entirely for the sake of observing. . . .

"If the adult world cannot somehow recognize that these primitive faculties represent final consummations to which the child is entitled as of right, it should at least take notice that the very same faculties constitute the core and marrow of the adult poet and the adult scientist.

The child's right to be a child, to ignore the clock, and to play heedlessly with words as though they were things and with things as though they were toys—this right is both morally valid and socially fruitful. And to the extent that this right may be recognized and protected, certain new duties necessarily fall on the members of the adult world." *The Moral Decision*, pp. 73–74.

NOTES TO CHAPTER EIGHT

1. Holmes, *The Common Law*, p. 1.
2. Harper, "Some Implications of Juristic Pragmatism," pp. 273–74.

Bibliography

Allen, Carleton Kemp. *Law in the Making.* Oxford: Clarendon Press, 1951 (5th ed.).

Aristotle. *Nicomachean Ethics,* Trans. W. D. Ross in *The Basic Works of Aristotle.* New York: Random House, 1941.

Austin, John. *The Province of Jurisprudence Determined.* New York: The Noonday Press, 1954.

Beard, Charles A. *An Economic Interpretation of the Constitution of the United States.* New York: Macmillan Co., 1913.

Berlin, Isaiah. "Equality," 56 Proceedings of the Aristotelian Society 301 (1956).

Black, Henry Campbell. *Handbook on the Law of Judicial Precedents; or The Science of Case Law.* St. Paul, Minn.: West Publishing Co., 1912.

Bodenheimer, Edgar. "Analytic Positivism, Legal Realism, and the Future of Legal Method," 44 Virginia Law Review 365 (1958).

———. "Law as Order and Justice," 6 Journal of Public Law 194 (1957).

Brandt, Richard B. *Ethical Theory.* Englewood Cliffs, New Jersey: Prentice-Hall, 1959.

Brown, Stuart M., Jr. "Utilitarianism and Moral Obligation," 61 Philosophical Review 299 (1952).

Cahn, Edmond N. *The Moral Decision.* Bloomington, Indiana: Indiana University Press, 1955.

———. *The Sense of Injustice.* New York: New York University Press, 1949.

Cardozo, Benjamin. *The Nature of the Judicial Process.* New Haven, Yale University Press, 1921.

———. *The Paradoxes of Legal Science.* New York: Columbia University Press, 1928.

Cohen, Morris. *Law and the Social Order.* New York: Harcourt, Brace, 1933.

Dewey, John. "Logical Method and Law," 10 Cornell Law Quarterly 17 (1924).

Dias, R. W. M., and G. B. J. Hughes. *Jurisprudence.* London: Butterworth and Co., 1957.

Dickinson, John. *Administrative Justice and the Supremacy of Law.* New York: Russell and Russell, 1959.

Ehrlich, Eugen. "Judicial Freedom of Decision: Its Principles and Objects," in *Science of Legal Method.* Modern Legal Philosophy Series. Boston: The Boston Book Co., 1917.

Ellenbogen, Henry. "The Doctrine of Stare Decisis and the Extent to Which It Should Be Applied," 20 Temple Law Quarterly 503 (1947).

Frank, Jerome. *Law and the Modern Mind.* New York: Tudor Publishing Co., 1936.

Fuller, Lon L. "Positivism and the Separation of Law and Morals—A Reply to Professor Hart," 71 Harvard Law Review 630 (1958).

Gmelin, Johann Georg. "Dialecticism and Technicality: The Need of Sociological Method," in *Science of Legal Method.* Modern Legal Philosophy Series. Boston: The Boston Book Co., 1917.

Goodhart, Arthur L. "Case Law in England and America," 15 Cornell Law Quarterly 173 (1930).

———. "Precedent in English and Continental Law," 50 Law Quarterly Review 40 (1934).

Harper, F. V. "Some Implications of Juristic Pragmatism," 39 International Journal of Ethics 269 (1929).

Hart, H. L. A. "Positivism and the Separation of Law and Morals," 71 Harvard Law Review 593 (1958).

———. "The Ascription of Responsibility and Rights," in *Logic and Language* (First Series), ed. by Antony Flew. Oxford: Basil Blackwell, 1952.

Hobbes, Thomas. *Leviathan.* Ed. Michael Oakeshott. Oxford: Basil Blackwell, 1957.

Hoebel, Edward Adamson. *The Law of Primitive Man.* Cambridge, Mass.: Harvard University Press, 1954.

Holdsworth, William S. "Case Law," 50 Law Quarterly Review 180 (1934).

Holmes, Oliver Wendell, Jr. *The Common Law.* Boston: Little, Brown, 1881.

——— "The Path of the Law," 10 Harvard Law Review 457 (1897).

Hume, David. *A Treatise of Human Nature.* Selby-Bigge ed. Oxford: Clarendon Press, 1888, 1958.

Hutcheson, Joseph C., Jr. "Lawyer's Law and the Little, Small Dice," 7 Tulane Law Review 1 (1932).

———. "The Judgment Intuitive: The Function of the 'Hunch' in Judicial Decision," 14 Cornell Law Quarterly 274 (1929).

Kantorowicz, Hermann. "Some Rationalism about Realism," 43 Yale Law Journal 1240 (1934).

Kelsen, Hans. "The Pure Theory of Law," 50 Law Quarterly Review 474 (1934).

Kocourek, Albert, and Harold Koven. "Renovation of the Common Law Through Stare Decisis," 29 Illinois Law Review 971 (1935).

Levi, Edward H. *An Introduction to Legal Reasoning.* Chicago: The University of Chicago Press, 1949.

Llewellyn, Karl. "Case Law," *Encyclopedia of the Social Sciences,* Vol. 3. New York: Macmillan Co., 1930.

————. *The Bramble Bush.* New York: Columbia University School of Law, 1930.

————. "The Rule of Law in Our Case-Law of Contract," 47 Yale Law Journal 1243 (1938).

————. "The Status of the Rule of Judicial Precedent," 14 University of Cincinnati Law Review 208 (1940).

McCloskey, H. J. "An Examination of Restricted Utilitarianism," 66 Philosophical Review 466 (1957).

McCormick, Charles T. *Handbook of the Law of Evidence.* St. Paul, Minn.: West Publishing Co., 1954.

————. *Handbook on the Law of Damages.* St. Paul, Minn.: West Publishing Co., 1935.

Melden, A. I. "Two Comments about Utilitarianism," 60 Philosophical Review 508 (1952).

Moschzisker, Robert von. "Stare Decisis in Courts of Last Resort," 37 Harvard Law Review 409 (1924).

Nowell-Smith, P. H. *Ethics.* Harmondsworth, Middlesex: Penguin Books, 1954.

Oliphant, Herman. "A Return to Stare Decisis," 14 American Bar Association Journal 71 (1928).

Patterson, Edwin. *Jurisprudence: Men and Ideas of the Law.* Brooklyn: The Foundation Press, Inc., 1953.

Phelps, Charles Edwards. *Elements of Judicial Equity.* Baltimore: King Brothers, 1890.

Pomeroy, John Norton. *A Treatise on Equity Jurisprudence.* San Francisco: Bancroft-Whitney Co.; Rochester, New York: The Lawyers Co-operative Publishing Co., 1918. (4th edition).

Pound, Cuthbert W. "Some Recent Phases of the Evolution of Case Law," 31 Yale Law Journal 361 (1922).

Pound, Roscoe, "Justice According to Law," 13 Columbia Law Review 696 (1913).

————. "Mechanical Jurisprudence," 8 Columbia Law Review 605 (1908).

————. "The Call for a Realist Jurisprudence," 44 Harvard Law Review 697 (1931).

————. "The Decadence of Equity," 5 Columbia Law Review 20 (1905).

————. "The Theory of Judicial Decision," 36 Harvard Law Review 641 (1923).

Radin, Max. "Case Law and Stare Decisis: Concerning *Prajudizienrecht in Amerika*," 33 Columbia Law Review 199 (1933).
———. *Law as Logic and Experience.* New Haven: Yale University Press, 1940.
———. "The Method of Law," Washington University Law Quarterly 471 (1950).
Rawls, John. "Two Concepts of Rules," 64 Philosophical Review 3 (1956).
Restatement of Contracts. St. Paul, Minn.: American Law Institute Publishers, 1932.
Ross, Alf. "The Value of Blood Tests as Evidence in Paternity Cases," 71 Harvard Law Review 466 (1958).
Rueff, Jacques. *From the Physical to the Social Sciences.* Introduction by Herman Oliphant and Abram Hewitt. Baltimore, Johns Hopkins Press, 1929.
Salmond, John W. *Jurisprudence.* London: Sweet and Maxwell, 1957. (11th ed.)
———. "The Theory of Judicial Precedents," 16 Law Quarterly Review 376 (1900).
Schoch, M. Magdalena (ed.). *The Jurisprudence of Interests.* Introduction by Lon L. Fuller. Cambridge, Mass.: Harvard University Press, 1948.
Smart, J. J. C. "Extreme and Restricted Utilitarianism," 6 Philosophical Quarterly 344 (1956).
Stoljar, S. J. "The Logical Status of a Legal Principle," 20 University of Chicago Law Review 181 (1953).
Stone, Julius. *The Province and Function of Law.* Cambridge, Mass.: Harvard University Press, 1950.
Toulmin, Stephen. *The Place of Reason in Ethics.* Cambridge, England: Cambridge University Press, 1953.
Urmson, J. O. "The Interpretation of the Philosophy of J. S. Mill," 3 Philosophical Quarterly 33 (1953).
Wade, H. W. R. "The Concept of Legal Certainty," 4 Modern Law Review 183 (1941).
Wechsler, Herbert. "Toward Neutral Principles of Constitutional Law," 73 Harvard Law Review 1 (1959).
Williams, Glanville L. "Language and the Law," 61, 62 Law Quarterly Review 71 (1945).

Index